MATT WAGNER
STEVEN T. SEAGLE
WRITERS

GUY DAVIS
ARTIST

DAVID HORNUNG
COLORIST

JOHN COSTANZA
LETTERER

Nanuet Public Library
149 Church Street
Nanuet, NY, 10954

SANDMAN MYSTERY THEATRE

- THE -
SCORPION

Karen Berger
VP-Executive Editor & Editor-original series

Shelly Roeberg
Associate Editor-original series

Scott Nybakken
Editor-collected edition

Robbin Brosterman
Senior Art Director

Paul Levitz
President & Publisher

Georg Brewer
VP-Design & DC Direct Creative

Richard Bruning
Senior VP-Creative Director

Patrick Caldon
Executive VP-Finance & Operations

Chris Caramalis
VP-Finance

John Cunningham
VP-Marketing

Terri Cunningham
VP-Managing Editor

Stephanie Fierman
Senior VP-Sales & Marketing

Alison Gill
VP-Manufacturing

Rich Johnson
VP-Book Trade Sales

Hank Kanalz
VP-General Manager, WildStorm

Lillian Laserson
Senior VP & General Counsel

Jim Lee
Editorial Director-WildStorm

Paula Lowitt
Senior VP-Business & Legal Affairs

David McKillips
VP-Advertising & Custom Publishing

John Nee
VP-Business Development

Gregory Noveck
Senior VP-Creative Affairs

Cheryl Rubin
Senior VP-Brand Management

Jeff Trojan
VP-Business Development, DC Direct

Bob Wayne
VP-Sales

SANDMAN MYSTERY THEATRE: THE SCORPION

Published by DC Comics. Cover and compilation copyright
© 2006 DC Comics. All Rights Reserved.

Originally published in single magazine form as SANDMAN
MYSTERY THEATRE 17-20. Copyright © 1994 DC Comics.
All Rights Reserved. All characters, their distinctive
likenesses and related elements featured in this publication
are trademarks of DC Comics. The stories, characters and
incidents featured in this publication are entirely fictional.
DC Comics does not read or accept unsolicited submissions
of ideas, stories or artwork.

DC Comics, 1700 Broadway, New York, NY 10019

A Warner Bros. Entertainment Company

Printed in Canada. First Printing.

ISBN: 1-4012-1040-6

ISBN 13: 978-1-4012-1040-3

Front and back cover photos by Gavin Wilson.

Original series covers by Gavin Wilson and Richard Bruning.

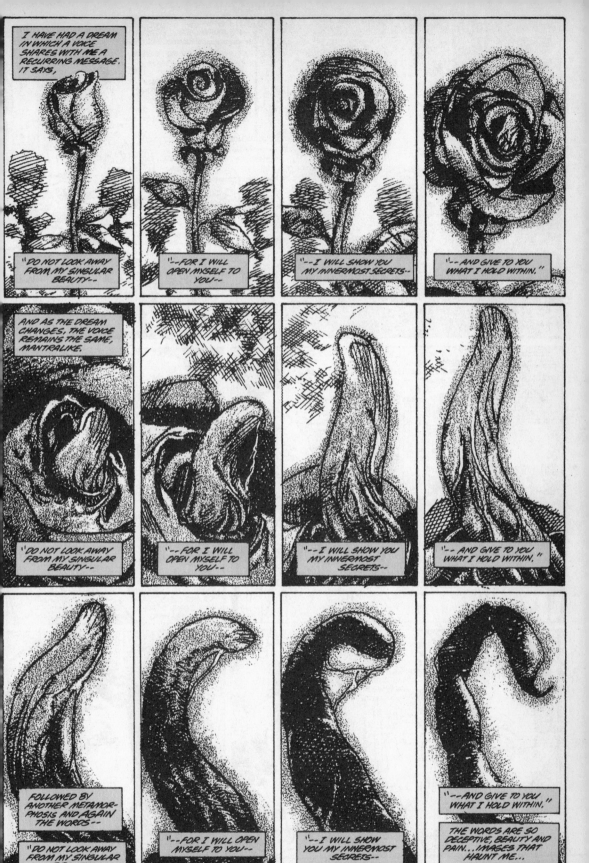

I HAVE HAD A DREAM IN WHICH A VOICE SHARES WITH ME A RECURRING MESSAGE. IT SAYS,

"DO NOT LOOK AWAY FROM MY SINGULAR BEAUTY--

"--FOR I WILL OPEN MYSELF TO YOU--

"--I WILL SHOW YOU MY INNERMOST SECRETS--

"--AND GIVE TO YOU WHAT I HOLD WITHIN."

AND AS THE DREAM CHANGES, THE VOICE REMAINS THE SAME, MANTRALIKE.

"DO NOT LOOK AWAY FROM MY SINGULAR BEAUTY--

"--FOR I WILL OPEN MYSELF TO YOU--

"--I WILL SHOW YOU MY INNERMOST SECRETS--

"--AND GIVE TO YOU WHAT I HOLD WITHIN."

FOLLOWED BY ANOTHER METAMOR-PHOSIS AND AGAIN THE WORDS--

"DO NOT LOOK AWAY FROM MY SINGULAR BEAUTY--

"--FOR I WILL OPEN MYSELF TO YOU--

"--I WILL SHOW YOU MY INNERMOST SECRETS--

"--AND GIVE TO YOU WHAT I HOLD WITHIN."

THE WORDS ARE SO DECEPTIVE, BEAUTY AND PAIN...IMAGES THAT HAUNT ME...

THE SCORPION

ACT ONE

...EVEN IN MY WAKING WORLD.

A WORLD WITH THE RUMOR OF WAR ON ITS LIPS. A NATION OF RAMPANT MOBSTER ACTIVITY AND REEKING STREET PEOPLE. A CITY IN WHICH BEAUTY SHOULD BE SNUFFED OUT THE INSTANT IT ARISES. AND YET--

--A PLACE WHERE BEAUTY...INEXPLICABLY... FLOURISHES.

UH--HERE'S YOUR--UH-- COFFEE, MA'AM. SIR? WE WERE OUT OF THE RHUBARB, SO I BROUGHT YOU--UH--A SLICE OF THE PUMPKIN, BUT IF IT'S NOT UH--TO YOUR LIKING, I CAN--

I MUST TELL YOU, DIAN, I REALLY ENJOYED OUR EVENING TOGETHER THE OTHER NIGHT.

YOU ENJOYED YOURSELF? BUT I WAS THE ONE-- WELL...I MEAN... YOU RAN AWAY SO QUICKLY.

IT WAS ALL VERY SPECIAL FOR ME, DIAN, BUT I DO HAVE TO APOLOGIZE...FOR NOT BEING THERE WHEN YOU WOKE.

AFTER YOU WENT TO SLEEP, I FELT I SHOULD ADJOURN TO MY STUDY. I--I WAS AFRAID THAT YOU MIGHT HAVE BEEN....OFFENDED.

OH MY, NO. QUITE THE OPPOSITE. I THINK I WAS JUST A BIT...DRAINED, WHAT WITH CAROL AND ALL, I JUST COULDN'T PUT THE PIECES IN PLACE--

--UNLIKE YOU WHO FIGURED IT OUT QUITE EASILY IT SEEMS. SOME "AMATEUR" DETECTIVE YOU TURNED OUT TO BE.

NO, I'M SURE IT'S PERFECTLY FINE. THANK YOU VERY MUCH.

AN AWKWARD BREAKFAST IS A FITTING CAP TO A TROUBLED NIGHT.

THERE IS A NEWFOUND INTIMACY BETWEEN DIAN AND ME NOW.

AND THOUGH IT LONGS TO FIND A VOICE, IT IS A DIFFICULT BREACH TO CROSS. BUT I BOTH NEED AND WANT TO MAKE THAT CROSSING.

OH, I WOULDN'T SAY I HAD THE WHOLE SOLUTION. IT NEVER CROSSED MY MIND THAT MADELINE--

LET'S NOT TALK ABOUT HER ANYMORE, WES. THAT'S AN UGLY CHAPTER THAT'S BEST LEFT CLOSED NOW.

I'M SORRY. I SUPPOSE IT IS ALL A LITTLE FRESH STILL.

SPEAKING OF FRESH, I WAS WONDERING WHEN WE COULD BE TOGETHER AGAIN--

--I'D LIKE TO GET YOU ALONE FOR A LITTLE WHILE SO I CAN...

...RETURN YOUR FAVOR...

WELL, YOU'VE CERTAINLY GOT MY ATTENTION, DIAN--

③

5

--BUT I HAVE AN *IMPOSSIBLY* BUSY WEEK AHEAD, *SO* BUSY IN FACT, THAT I DON'T EVEN THINK I'M GOING TO MAKE IT TO THE BUSTER CALHOUN CHARITY CONCERT THIS EVENING--

BUSTER CALHOUN? THE WESTERN FILM STAR? OH, DADDY *LOVES* HIM!

REALLY? THEN IT'S *PERFECT.* YOU'LL HAVE *MY* TICKETS, TWO SEATS, FRONT ROW CENTER.

OH NO, WESLEY, WE *COULDN'T.*

I *INSIST.*

THE CHARITY FUNCTION IS MERELY A RUSE FOR THE SPONSORS TO CONTACT INVESTORS FOR AN OIL DEAL THEY HAVE GOING. I'M NOT THE *LEAST* BIT INTERESTED SO TAKE THEM.

OTHERWISE, THEY'LL JUST GO TO WASTE

WHY ARE YOU THE SWEETEST MAN IN NEW YORK CITY? DADDY WILL BE *SO* THRILLED.

ACTUALLY, THE TICKETS ARE FOR YOU *AND* YOUR FATHER, BUT *THIS...* IS JUST FOR YOU.

DIAN IS SO CARING. YET, FOR ALL HER CHARITY WORK, SHE DOESN'T SEEM TO REALIZE HOW LUDICROUS A HIGH TICKET GALA IS IN THE EBBING TIDES OF THE DEPRESSION.

AN ORIGAMI ROSE? IT'S LOVELY...

BUT NEXT TO YOU IT'S ONLY PAPER.

--AT TIMES WHEN FATHERS DIG DINNER FROM GARBAGE CONTAINERS WE DRESS UP IN OUR SUNDAY'S FINEST AND PAY LUDICROUS AMOUNTS OF MONEY TO HEAR THE NASAL MEWLINGS OF A WESTERN SIMPLETON. BEAUTY AND PAIN.

④

♪--and thaaat--♪ was the ennnd--of Black Heart Bart!

THANK YEW, LADIES AN' GENTS! I'M BUSTER CALHOUN AND THAT'S THE SHOW FER THIS EVENING! YEEEEE-HA!

OH, THAT WAS TERRIFIC. HE WAS JUST TERRIFIC! DON'T YOU THINK, DIAN?

HE WAS DEFINITELY--

IT WAS SUPER, JUST SUPER!

OH! THERE'S THE MAYOR. WE SHOULD SAY HELLO.

MR. MAYOR? MR. MAYOR?

LARRY! HOW ARE YOU DOING? I MUST BE PAYING YOU TOO MUCH IF YOU CAN AFFORD TICKETS TO AN EVENT LIKE THIS.

OH, NO, MR. MAYOR. YOU'RE NOT OVERPAYING ME AT ALL. WESLEY DODDS GAVE ME HIS TICKETS AS A GIFT. I LOVE THAT COWBOY MUSIC, AND ESPECIALLY BUSTER CALHOUN!

OH, YES, I WAS WONDERING WHY DODDS WASN'T HERE. THAT MAN SEEMS TO MISS EVERY-THING THESE DAYS.

I WAS HOPING TO INTRODUCE HIM TO THE MEN WHO PUT ON TONIGHT'S SHOW, BUT I GUESS--

IF IT'S NOT AN IMPOSITION, SIR, I'D BE HONORED TO MEET THEM, AND TO BE ABLE TO THANK THEM PERSONALLY.

WELL, SINCE YOU *ARE* HERE IN WESLEY'S *PLACE*--AHURUMPH--GENTLEMEN, I'D LIKE TO INTRODUCE YOU TO DISTRICT ATTORNEY LAWRENCE BELMONT. LAWRENCE--THE ENTREPRENEURS BEHIND TONIGHT'S EVENT--

MR. EMMANUEL LANE--

HELLO.

-- MR. HELMET RUMMEL--

A PLEASURE.

--AND MR. KARL DECHERT.

EH? WHO IS DIS?

WELL, IT'S CERTAINLY A PLEASURE TO MEET YOU, BUT WE WERE JUST LEAVING. I'M AFRAID WE ALL FIND CROWDS MORE THAN A LITTLE...TAXING.

WELL SPOKEN, LET'S *DO* BE ON OUR WAY.

DON'T WORRY ABOUT IT, GENTLEMEN, THEY'RE *ALWAYS* LIKE THAT.

UH... I JUST WANTED TO EXPRESS MY THANKS FOR YOUR ARRANGING TO GET BUSTER IN HERE, HE WAS *GREAT.*

YEAH, TANKS. GOODNIGHT.

DID I SAY SOMETHING TO *OFFEND* THEM?

AH, MR. CUTLER. I HOPE WE DIDN'T INSULT YOUR SENIOR PARTNERS.

INSULT THEM? GENTLEMEN OF *THEIR* STATURE OFTEN FORGET THE INTRICACIES OF COURTESY.

AND WHO IS THIS *RADIANT* YOUNG WOMAN IN YOUR COMPANY, GENTLEMEN?

OH, THIS IS MY DAUGHTER... MISS DIAN BELMONT.

A *PLEASURE,* MR. CUTLER. I'VE HEARD A LOT ABOUT YOU.

8

I'LL DO MY BEST TO DISPEL IT, AND PLEASE, CALL ME STEPHEN.

ALLOW ME TO INTRODUCE MY DAUGHTER, AND RIGHT-HAND GAL, CASSANDRA, AND THE GATECRASHER NEXT TO HER IS OUR ADVERTISING MAN, TERRY STETSON.

HELLO.

A PLEASURE TO MEET YOU, SIR.

YOU KNOW, I'VE BEEN THINKING ABOUT A CAMPAIGN FOR THE CITY HERE, NEW IDEA, ADVERTISING A WHOLE CITY TO THE--

UH--

YOU WORK FOR YOUR FATHER, CASSANDRA?

WITH HIM, ACTUALLY. I'M IN CHARGE OF OUR EUROPEAN DISTRIBUTION. OF COURSE, WITH THE OIL SITUATION BEING WHAT IT IS OVER THERE THESE DAYS, IT'S ALMOST TOO MUCH FOR EVEN ME TO KEEP TRACK OF.

LARRY, TELL ME, WHAT BRINGS OUR DISTRICT ATTORNEY TO A HIGHBROW AFFAIR LIKE THIS?

I'M STANDING IN FOR WESLEY DODDS, ACTUALLY.

REALLY? AND WHERE IS DODDS TONIGHT? I HAD HOPED TO DISCUSS SOME INVESTMENT POSSIBILITIES WITH HIM. NOW I'M GOING TO HAVE TO TRACK HIM DOWN.

OH, UM...HE HAD SOME WORK TO FINISH. THAT'S WESLEY FOR YOU. SOMETIMES, HE'S JUST ALL WORK AND NO PLAY.

SOLITUDE...

⑦

--I SEEK A PERFECT QUIETNESS--

--THOUGH IT IS IMPOSSIBLE TO SHUT OFF THE WORLD I SEE COLLAPSING AROUND ME--

--A WORLD THAT HAS BEEN KNOCKED OUT OF BALANCE.

EUROPE IS DESTROYING ITSELF AND THE ASIAN ECONOMIES ARE CRUMBLING --EVEN AS AMERICA CONTINUES TO DREAM.

I SEE THE VALUES OF DECENCY AND HONESTY BEING SLOWLY EATEN AWAY BY SOME PARASITIC COMPULSION--

AND ALL THE WHILE THE PEOPLE IN MY LIFE PRETEND THAT ALL IS AS IT WAS IN THE GOOD OLD DAYS.

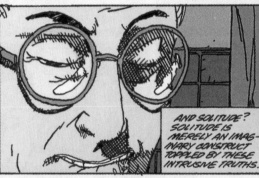

AND SOLITUDE? SOLITUDE IS MERELY AN IMAGINARY CONSTRUCT TOPPLED BY THESE INTRUSIVE TRUTHS.

TRUTHS WHICH WILL ELUDE ME AS WELL WHEN I TRY TO EXPLAIN THIS SCAR TO DIAN. HOW WILL I EXPLAIN IT? ANY WAY I CAN, I'M SURE.

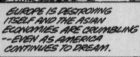

SO MUCH OF MY TIME SEEMS TO BE DEVOTED TO TRYING TO EXPLAIN AWAY WHAT I REALLY AM.

PARK IT, PROBST. MISS BONBA UND I VILL NOT BE GOINK BACK OUT.

YES, MR. DECHERT.

TSK TSK TSK TSK--

--TSK TSK TSK.

YOU KNOW... YOU HAFF BEEN A NAUGHTY LITTLE GIRL TONIGHT, SABINA.

11

OH, REALLY, MR. DECHERT?

YA, YOU HAFF. I ZAW YOU MAKINK EYES AT YOUNG HERR SHTAMPER.

VAS HE MAKINK EYES AT YOU?

DID HE TRY TO--

NUH--

--TRY TO PUT HIZ HANDS ON YOUR TITTIES? ON YOUR BOTTOM?

SPLOIP

DID HE, SABINA?

TELL ME.

I SUPPOSE HE DID, MR. DECHERT.

YA, PLEASE, I HAFF TOLD YOU... CALL ME POPPY.

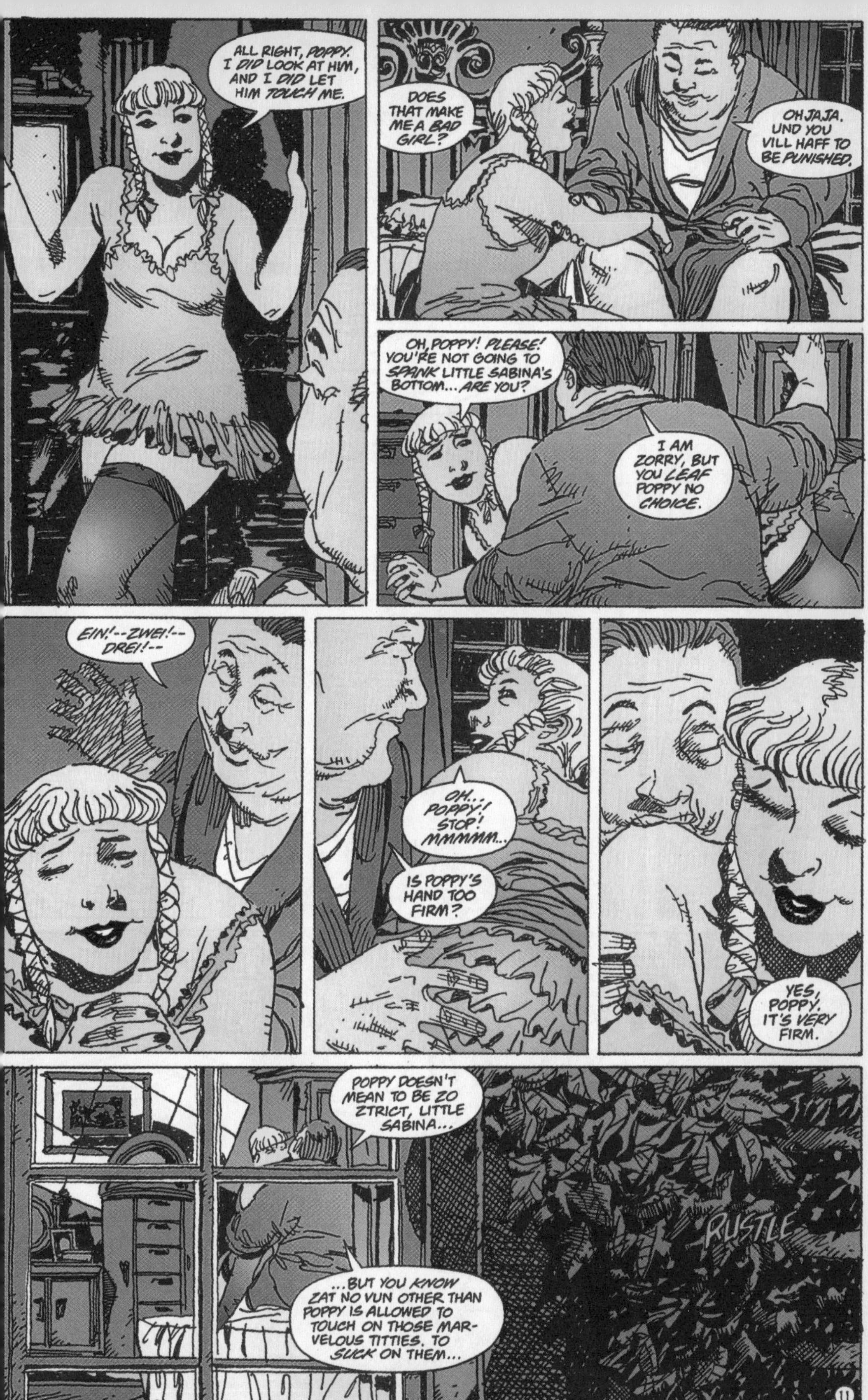
ALL RIGHT, POPPY. I DID LOOK AT HIM, AND I DID LET HIM TOUCH ME.
DOES THAT MAKE ME A BAD GIRL?
OH JAJA. UND YOU VILL HAFF TO BE PUNISHED.
OH, POPPY! PLEASE! YOU'RE NOT GOING TO SPANK LITTLE SABINA'S BOTTOM... ARE YOU?
I AM ZORRY, BUT YOU LEAF POPPY NO CHOICE.
EIN!--ZWEI!--DREI!--
OH... POPPY! STOP! MMMMMM...
IS POPPY'S HAND TOO FIRM?
YES, POPPY. IT'S VERY FIRM.
POPPY DOESN'T MEAN TO BE ZO ZTRICT, LITTLE SABINA...
RUSTLE
...BUT YOU KNOW ZAT NO VUN OTHER THAN POPPY IS ALLOWED TO TOUCH ON THOSE MARVELOUS TITTIES. TO SUCK ON THEM...
11

POPPY? I DIDN'T LET HIM TOUCH *EVERY* PART. I SAVED A SPECIAL PART JUST-- FOR-- YOU.

HMMMM... VELL ZEN, POPPY FORGIVES YOU, LITTLE SABINA, POPPY--

NNH! POPPY FOR-- UNH! GIVES YOU--

POPPY-- NNH!-- FOR--

SWK--

UNH!-- GIVES--

CRAC-

UNNGH!

OCK! CHEESUS!

POPPY?

POPPY?

UNGAAFF--

FUNGH! URK--

POPPY? POPPY? EEEEEEE!

12

DON'T TOUCH HIM YET, EDDIE, I WANT TO GET A SHOT OF HIS *BACK*--

LISTEN, HONEY. NO POINT IN CLAMMIN' UP. WHY DON'T YOU JUST TELL ME WHAT YOU DID TO MR. DECHERT THERE?

I DIDN'T DO *ANYTHING* TO HIM.

LOOK, SISTER, JUST *LOOKIN'* AT THE GUY I KNOW YOU WAS DOIN' *SOMETHIN'* WITH HIM.

HONEST, I WASN'T--

TOOTS, IT'S NO BIG MYSTERY THAT YOU'RE DECHERT'S TWIST, SO IF *THAT'S* WHAT YOU'RE TRYIN' TO HIDE, JUST *SAVE* IT.

I'M *TELLING* YOU, I DIDN'T HAVE ANYTHING TO *DO* WITH THIS.

THEN YOU'D BETTER RAT AND *QUICK.* HM...

HE WAS *SPANKING* ME, HE WAS *ON* ME, THEN HE FELL OVER. I JUST FIGURED HE HAD A HEART ATTACK. THAT'S *ALL.*

GOT YOUR KILLER THERE, BURKE?

NAH. NO MOTIVE, AND BESIDES--

--I CHECKED UNDER HER NAILS... NO BLOOD.

WHATEVER MADE THIS MARK, IT *WASN'T* A STREET GIRL GETTING TOO WILD WITH AN OLD MAN.

13

I TELL YA, ROSS, THIS DAMN TOWN IS GETTING WEIRDER BY THE DAY.

I KNOW WHAT YOU MEAN, BURKE. ANY NEW NEWS ON THAT DECHERT KILLING?

YEAH, WORD'S IN FROM THE CORONER. POISON. FAST-ACTING, LETHAL SHIT TOO... KICKED IN ALMOST INSTANTLY.

SAYS HERE THE POISON GOT IN THROUGH THE WOUND ON HIS BACK? SO THAT *MUST* MEAN IT WAS THE GIRL.

NAH, SHE ISN'T OUR FINGER. WHOEVER *PUT* THE CUT IN DECHERT'S BACK IS WHO WE'RE LOOKIN' FOR. AND GET *THIS*--

--THE M.E. SAYS HE THINKS THE WEAPON MIGHT 'A' BEEN A BULL WHIP. CAN YOU BELIEVE THAT SHIT?

DECHERT WAS A MAJOR MOVER IN THIS CITY: OLD MONEY. TRADERS BEFORE THE INDUSTRIAL REVOLUTION, TEXTILES AND OIL SINCE.

DECHERT WAS ANYTHING BUT A COMPASSIONATE EMPLOYER. BRUTAL BOSSES HAVE ANY NUMBER OF ENEMIES. NOT TO MENTION THE CITY OFFICIALS ON DECHERT'S PRIVATE PAYROLL WHO MIGHT HAVE BEEN NERVOUS ABOUT EXPOSURE.

14

REGARDLESS OF WHO DID HIM IN, IT ISN'T OFTEN THAT SOMEBODY SO HIGH UP IN THIS CITY--

GENTLEMEN, CASSANDRA, BEFORE WE START THIS MEETING, I THINK I SHOULD SAY A FEW WORDS ABOUT OUR LONGTIME COLLEAGUE NOW DEPARTED.

--TAKES THAT KIND OF FALL.

HARRY WAS A PIVOTAL FORCE IN THIS COMPANY, AND HIS PASSING SHOULD SERVE TO REMIND US ALL THAT LIFE IS A FLEETING, DELICATE THING.

HIS STRONG SENSE OF DISCIPLINE SHALL ALWAYS REMAIN A FOUNDATION FOR THIS COMPANY IN EVERY ENDEAVOR.

A MOMENT OF SILENCE, PLEASE.

GOOD.

THAT SAID, I THINK IT'S TIME WE GOT BACK TO BUSINESS AND TURNED THE MEETING OVER TO TERRY.

THANKS, MR. CUTLER. MR. DECHERT'S PASSING WAS A SHOCK, BUT IT CAN'T STOP THE WHEELS OF HIGH FINANCE, SO ON THE BRIGHTER SIDE OF THINGS-- THE BUSTER CALHOUN SHOW WAS A HUGE SUCCESS.

15

COMPASSIONATE LITTLE SON OF A BITCH, ISN'T HE?

DID THIS LITTLE COWBOY STUNT BRING US ANY CLOSER TO OUR REAL GOAL, STETSON?

YESSIR. NOT ONLY ARE WE BACK IN THE PUBLIC EYE IN A POSITIVE WAY, SIR, BUT WE LINED UP OVER 30 NEW CONTRIBUTORS FOR THE FOREIGN OIL REFINERY DEPOSITORY PROJECT, OR THE F.O.R.D. AS I'M NOW CALLING IT-- HEH HEH, LITTLE JOKE THERE--

YES, VERY LITTLE. WHERE DOES THAT LEAVE US IN TERMS OF FUNDING?

IT IS MY OPINION THAT WE ARE SHORT ONLY ONE MAJOR INVESTOR. WESLEY DODDS SEEMS TO BE THE MOST LIKELY TO BE ABLE TO FORWARD THE BALANCE OF THE START-UP CAPITAL.

I'VE HEARD HE'S A TOUGH NUT TO CRACK WHEN IT COMES TO GETTING MONEY AWAY FROM HIS HOLDINGS.

TRUE ENOUGH, AND THAT'S WHY I'M RECOMMENDING THAT YOU AND I, MR. CUTLER, PURSUE AN AGGRESSIVE COURT-SHIP FOR...

I DON'T WANT TO APPEAR TOO VORACIOUS FOLLOWING THE COMPANY'S RECENT TRAGEDY. I SUGGEST THAT CASSANDRA TAKE MY PLACE.

CASS-- WITH ALL DUE RESPECT, MR. CUTLER, THIS IS A MAN'S GAME. WE CAN'T BE PLAYIN' AROUND WHILE THE WINDOW'S OPEN.

WHERE THERE'S AN OPEN WINDOW, THERE'S USUALLY A DRAFT, MR. STETSON. YOU AND ME. TAKE IT OR LEAVE IT.

HEH. OKAY... YOU WIN, MISS CUTLER. LET'S HOPE YOU'RE AS LUCKY WITH WESLEY DODDS.

16

18

ONE OF THE PROBLEMS WITH HAVING INHERITED MY FATHER'S INTERESTS IS THAT I INHERITED THE SOCIAL RESPONSIBILITIES ATTACHED TO THEM AS WELL.

IT'S NOT THAT I HATE BEING WEALTHY. ONLY A FOOL WOULD DENY THE OBVIOUS ADVANTAGES. STILL, MY FORTUNE DOES OFTEN BECOME A PUBLIC ALBATROSS. ONE I WOULD JUST AS SOON REMOVE FOREVER.

WELL, AT LEAST THE RIDE OVER HERE WAS NICE.

WES...IT'S FINE. REALLY. YOU'VE GOTTEN ALL WORKED UP OVER THIS DINNER AND I DON'T UNDERSTAND WHY. I DIDN'T THINK WE'D EVEN SEE EACH OTHER TONIGHT, AND NOW WE'LL BE HAVING A FULL EVENING TOGETHER.

YES... JUST YOU AND ME... AND THE CUTLER CUTTHROATS. I WISH IT COULD HAVE BEEN JUST US, BUT I REALLY COULDN'T THINK OF ANOTHER DELICATE WAY TO BACK OUT OF THIS.

BETTER TO JUST HEAR THEM OUT, DECLINE, AND HOPEFULLY BE DONE WITH THEM FOR ANOTHER YEAR OR SO. I JUST HOPE IT ISN'T TOO DREADFUL FOR YOU--

IT'S ALL RIGHT, WES. ANY TIME SPENT WITH YOU WILL BE EXCITING, I'M SURE.

DID I MENTION THIS WAS A MEETING TO DISCUSS AN OIL IMPORTING DEAL?

OH...DO YOU THINK OUR CAB HAS ALREADY LEFT?

HEH. OKAY, OKAY... I'LL STOP.

RIGHT THIS WAY, PLEASE.

WESLEY, GLAD YOU COULD MAKE IT. WE MISSED YOU AT THE BUSTER CALHOUN SHOW.

DON'T TAKE IT PERSONALLY, I ALWAYS HAVE TROUBLE MAKING IT TO FUNDRAISERS.

SHARP! VERY SHARP! I LIKE A MAN WITH WIT.

ALLOW ME TO INTRODUCE MY... FRIEND, MISS DIAN BELMONT. DIAN THIS IS--

WE'VE ALREADY MET.

17

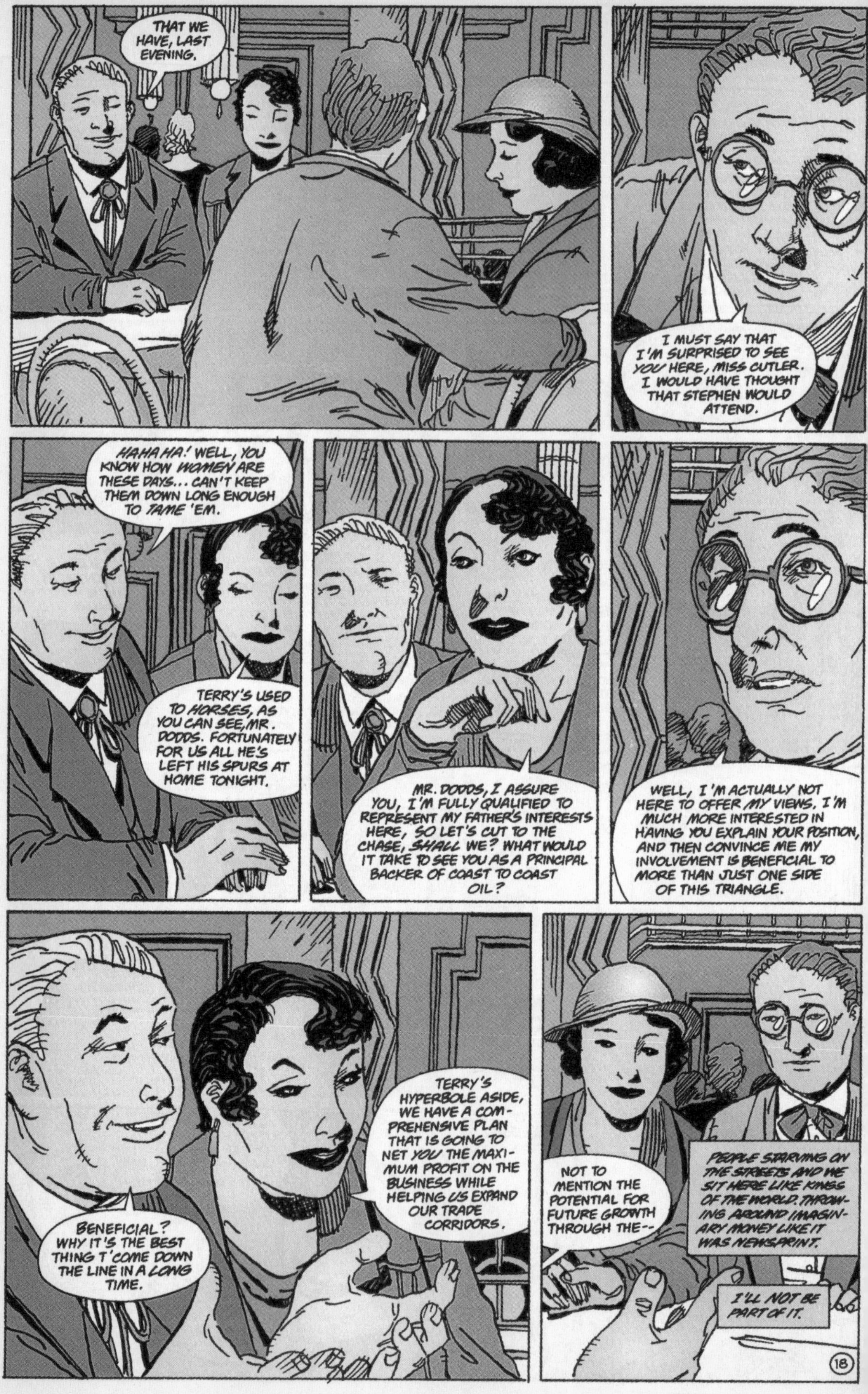
THAT WE HAVE, LAST EVENING.
I MUST SAY THAT I'M SURPRISED TO SEE YOU HERE, MISS CUTLER. I WOULD HAVE THOUGHT THAT STEPHEN WOULD ATTEND.
HAHAHA! WELL, YOU KNOW HOW WOMEN ARE THESE DAYS... CAN'T KEEP THEM DOWN LONG ENOUGH TO TAME 'EM.
TERRY'S USED TO HORSES, AS YOU CAN SEE, MR. DODDS. FORTUNATELY FOR US ALL HE'S LEFT HIS SPURS AT HOME TONIGHT.
MR. DODDS, I ASSURE YOU, I'M FULLY QUALIFIED TO REPRESENT MY FATHER'S INTERESTS HERE, SO LET'S CUT TO THE CHASE, SHALL WE? WHAT WOULD IT TAKE TO SEE YOU AS A PRINCIPAL BACKER OF COAST TO COAST OIL?
WELL, I'M ACTUALLY NOT HERE TO OFFER MY VIEWS. I'M MUCH MORE INTERESTED IN HAVING YOU EXPLAIN YOUR POSITION, AND THEN CONVINCE ME MY INVOLVEMENT IS BENEFICIAL TO MORE THAN JUST ONE SIDE OF THIS TRIANGLE.
BENEFICIAL? WHY IT'S THE BEST THING T'COME DOWN THE LINE IN A LONG TIME.
TERRY'S HYPERBOLE ASIDE, WE HAVE A COMPREHENSIVE PLAN THAT IS GOING TO NET YOU THE MAXIMUM PROFIT ON THE BUSINESS WHILE HELPING US EXPAND OUR TRADE CORRIDORS.
NOT TO MENTION THE POTENTIAL FOR FUTURE GROWTH THROUGH THE--
PEOPLE STARVING ON THE STREETS AND WE SIT HERE LIKE KINGS OF THE WORLD. THROWING AROUND IMAGINARY MONEY LIKE IT WAS NEWSPRINT.
I'LL NOT BE PART OF IT.
18

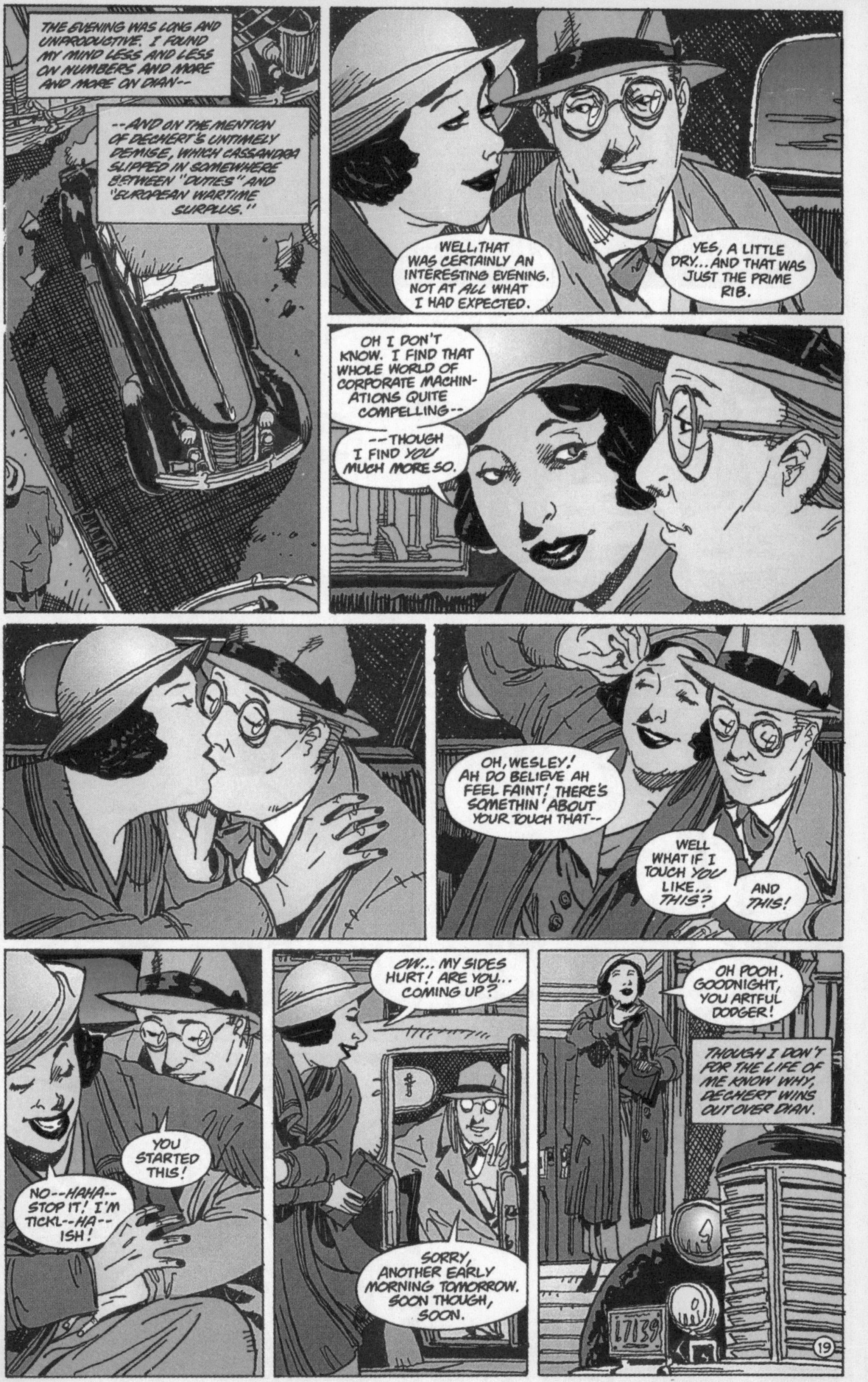
THE EVENING WAS LONG AND UNPRODUCTIVE. I FOUND MY MIND LESS AND LESS ON NUMBERS AND MORE AND MORE ON DIAN--
--AND ON THE MENTION OF DECHERT'S UNTIMELY DEMISE, WHICH CASSANDRA SLIPPED IN SOMEWHERE BETWEEN "DUTIES" AND "EUROPEAN WARTIME SURPLUS."
WELL, THAT WAS CERTAINLY AN INTERESTING EVENING. NOT AT ALL WHAT I HAD EXPECTED.
YES, A LITTLE DRY... AND THAT WAS JUST THE PRIME RIB.
OH I DON'T KNOW. I FIND THAT WHOLE WORLD OF CORPORATE MACHIN-ATIONS QUITE COMPELLING--
--THOUGH I FIND YOU MUCH MORE SO.
OH, WESLEY! AH DO BELIEVE AH FEEL FAINT! THERE'S SOMETHIN' ABOUT YOUR TOUCH THAT--
WELL WHAT IF I TOUCH YOU LIKE... THIS?
AND THIS!
YOU STARTED THIS!
NO--HAHA-- STOP IT! I'M TICKL--HA-- ISH!
OW... MY SIDES HURT! ARE YOU... COMING UP?
SORRY, ANOTHER EARLY MORNING TOMORROW. SOON THOUGH, SOON.
OH POOH. GOODNIGHT, YOU ARTFUL DODGER!
THOUGH I DON'T FOR THE LIFE OF ME KNOW WHY, DECHERT WINS OUT OVER DIAN.
17139
19

THIS TIME IT'S MY *PRIVATE* RESPONSIBILITIES THAT TAKE PRECEDENCE OVER MY IMMEDIATE DESIRES.

WELL, HERE WE ARE THEN.

THANKS FOR THE LIFT HOME, TERRY.

IT WAS MY *PLEASURE,* CASSIE.

CASSANDRA?

I WANT YOU TO KNOW THAT I MEAN THAT, *REALLY,* I DO.

TERRY... I *UH...*

YEAH?

I THINK WE... WORKED WELL TOGETHER TONIGHT. DODDS WILL ALMOST CERTAINLY GO FOR THE DEAL NOW.

YEAH... YEAH, I'M *SURE* HE WILL TOO.

YES... WELL, GOODNIGHT.

YOU'RE A *SLICK* ONE, TERRY. I'LL GIVE YOU THAT. A LITTLE PRIMITIVE PERHAPS, BUT SLICK.

I'LL TAKE THAT AS A COMPLIMENT.

YOU CAN TAKE THAT ANY WAY YOU WANT TO TAKE IT. GOODNIGHT.

20

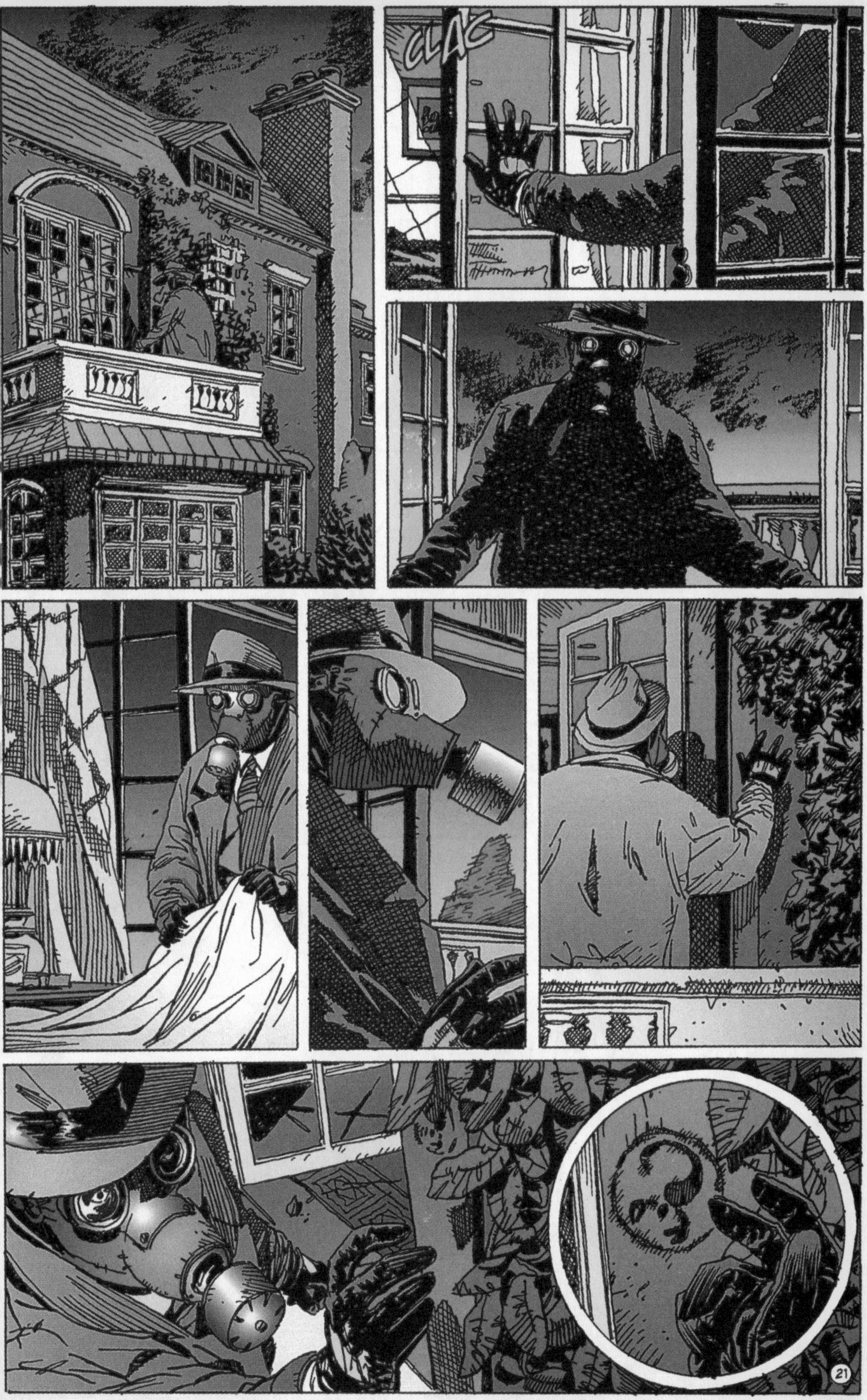
CLAC
21

DOMINICK! WHERE IN HELL ARE YOU?

I'M SO SORRY, MR. RUMMEL. I DIDN'T HEAR YOU COME IN--

NO, OBVIOUSLY YOU DIDN'T. I'M GOING TO MY STUDY. I'LL HAVE COFFEE AND BRANDY THERE, IN TEN MINUTES.

YES, SIR--

AND I WANT MY BATH DRAWN BY ELEVEN THIRTY. NOW BE OFF.

YES, SIR.

I SHOULD HAVE KNOWN A SPIC WOULD NEVER AMOUNT TO A MINUTE'S WORTH OF USE AROUND HERE.

...NOT AROUND WHEN YOU NEED HIM...

TOK

...UNDERFOOT WHEN YOU DON'T...

CLAC

HOW'S ONE EXPECTED TO COPE IN A WORLD FILLED WITH SUCH IDIOTS?!

22

25

NANUET PUBLIC LIBRARY
149 CHURCH STREET
NANUET, NEW YORK 10954
845-623-4281

I WANT MY HASSOCK! OH GOOD, YOU'VE GOT IT. GOOD.

DID YOU KNOW, DOMINICK, THAT MY PARTNER, MR. DECHERT, WAS *KILLED* IN HIS HOME LAST NIGHT? GO AHEAD, YOU MAY ANSWER ME.

NO, I DID *NOT* KNOW THAT, SIR. WAS IT NATURAL CAUSES?

YES...IT WAS NATURAL. HE *DIED.* RUB MY FEET.

SO *ANYHOW,* THEY FOUND HIM IN HIS APARTMENT WITH A-- TAKE THE BOOT OFF FIRST GODDAMMIT!

I'M TRYING TO--

TRY HARDER!

I *THINK* IT'S COMING--

CHUP

DAMN IT! YOU'VE MADE ME SPILL ON MYSELF!

WHAC WHAC WHAC WHAC WHACK

YOU-- STUPID-- IGNORANT-- BASTARD

CRAC-

AH!

SHIT! WHAT DID YOU DO TO ME?

24

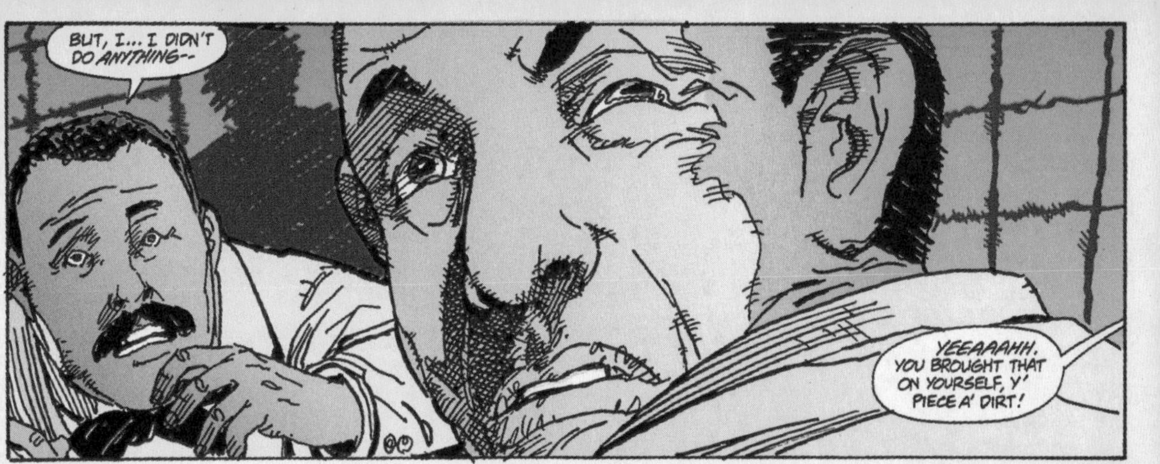
BUT, I... I DIDN'T DO ANYTHING--
YEEAAAHH. YOU BROUGHT THAT ON YOURSELF, Y' PIECE A' DIRT!

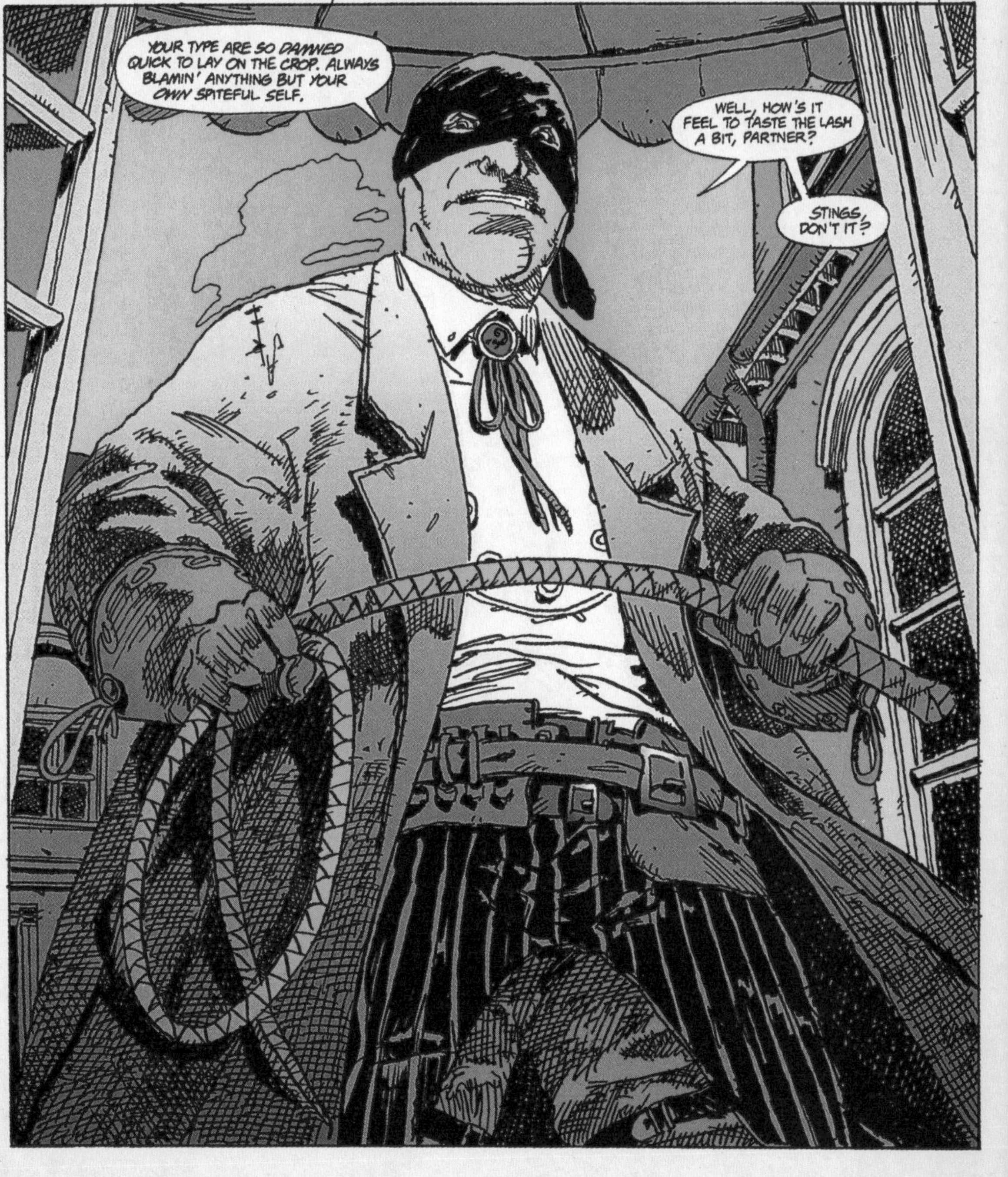
YOUR TYPE ARE SO DAMNED QUICK TO LAY ON THE CROP. ALWAYS BLAMIN' ANYTHING BUT YOUR OWN SPITEFUL SELF.
WELL, HOW'S IT FEEL TO TASTE THE LASH A BIT, PARTNER?
STINGS, DON'T IT?

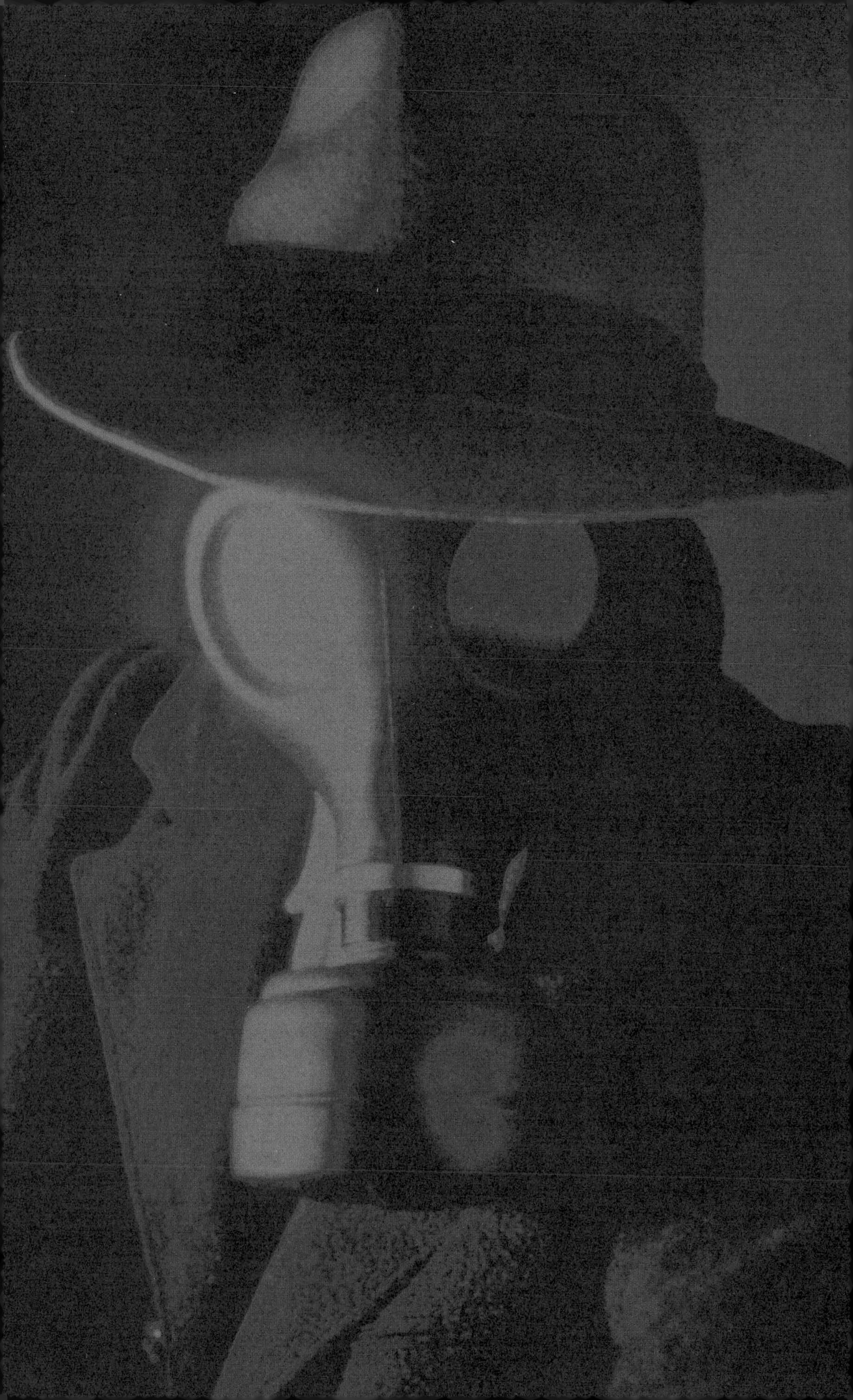

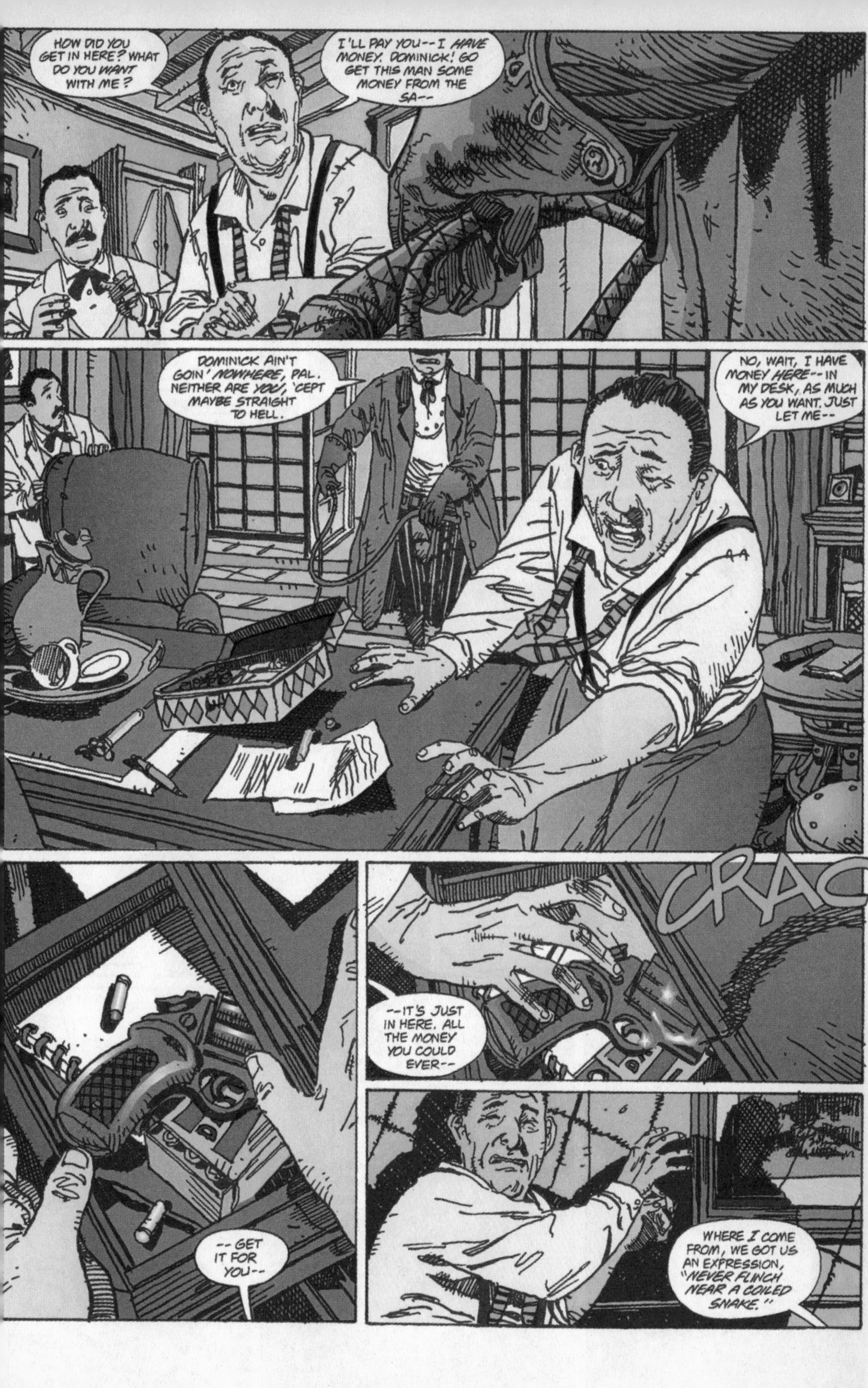
HOW DID YOU GET IN HERE? WHAT DO YOU WANT WITH ME?
I'LL PAY YOU-- I HAVE MONEY. DOMINICK! GO GET THIS MAN SOME MONEY FROM THE SA--
DOMINICK AIN'T GOIN' NOWHERE, PAL. NEITHER ARE YOU, 'CEPT MAYBE STRAIGHT TO HELL.
NO, WAIT, I HAVE MONEY HERE-- IN MY DESK, AS MUCH AS YOU WANT. JUST LET ME--
-- GET IT FOR YOU--
CRAC
--IT'S JUST IN HERE. ALL THE MONEY YOU COULD EVER--
WHERE I COME FROM, WE GOT US AN EXPRESSION, "NEVER FLINCH NEAR A COILED SNAKE."

YOU *HEARD* THAT ONE BEFORE?

NO! PLEASE, I *WASN'T*-- I *DIDN'T* REMEMBER THAT GUN BEING IN THE DRAWER--

DON'T CARE MUCH FOR *LIARS* EITHER, OLD MAN.

WHERE I'M FROM, WE *HANG* LIARS.

STOP! PLEASE, I'LL DO *ANYTHING* YOU WANT. GIVE YOU *ANYTHING* YOU WANT, JUST--

WHAT I *WANT* IS TO SEE YOU FALL.

THUD

UNH!

HOW'S IT FEEL T'BE ON THE *GROUND* WHERE YOU TRY TO KEEP THE REST OF THE WORLD, RUMMEL?

UNNH...

HOW'S IT FEEL TO BEND *YOUR* BACK IN PAIN FOR A CHANGE? HUH?

WHUMP

AAAAF!

WHAT'S IT LIKE T'BE *UNDER* SOMEONE'S *BOOTS* AND KNOW THAT *NOTHIN'* YOU CAN DO IS GONNA GET YOU *OVER* THOSE BOOTS?

STOP IT! ST--

2

THUD
THUD
THUD

--AAAAAH!

IT *DOESN'T* STOP, RUMMEL. THAT'S THE PROBLEM.

THE PEOPLE WITH THE POWER-- *BORN* WITH IT, MIND YOU-- THEY *START* ON TOP, AND THEY *END* ON TOP.

...DOMINICK-- NUCK-- H--HELP ME...

YOU SON OF A BITCH! WHY ARE YOU *HURTING* ME? WHAT DO YOU WANT?

WHAT DO I WANT? TELL YA WHAT I *DON'T* WANT. I DON'T WANT YOUR *MONEY*. NOSIREE BOB. DON'T *WANT* IT...DON'T *NEED* IT, GOT ENOUGH MONEY.

WHAT I WANT IS *YOU* AND EVERY OTHER RICH BASTARD *LIKE* YOU ON YOUR KNEES.

AND IF I HAVE T' KILL EVERY LAST ONE O' YOU T' PUT YOU THERE--

ERAC

--THEN, BY GOD, I'LL DO IT.

AAAAAAAAAA!

--I'M SORRY, MR. RUMMEL-- SORRY-- SO SORRY--

HE WOULDN'T 'A BEEN SORRY IF YOUR PLACES WERE SWITCHED, BET ON IT.

③

THE SCORPION
ACT TWO

CHRIST! BAD ENOUGH WE GOT THIS FREAK STORM, NOW WE GOTTA START RUNNIN' DOWN *SUSPECTS* IN IT--

OKAY, KLEIN, I'M *HERE*. WHAT'S TH' RUNDOWN? SAME AS THE LAST ONE?

NOT QUITE, LT. BURKE. THERE ARE SIMILARITIES, BUT THERE ARE *ALSO* SOME MAJOR DIFFERENCES.

GIMME TH' DIFFERENCES FIRST.

...THIS GUY PART OF THAT SAME COMPANY?

OH YEAH, SAME COMPANY ALL RIGHT. EVEN THE SAME...

WELL, AS YOU CAN TELL BY THE SKIN DISCOLORATION MR. RUMMEL WAS SEVERELY TRAUMATIZED. FROM THE SHAPE AND DEPTH OF THE CONTUSIONS, I'D SAY HE WAS MOST LIKELY KICKED.

HOW MUCH DOES THE CITY PAY YOU TO STATE THE *OBVIOUS*, KLEIN!

I'M SORRY, LIEUTENANT, BUT YOU ASKED ME-- WELL, ANYHOW--

--WE HAVE A SET OF IMPACT MARKS VERY SIMILAR TO THOSE FOUND IN THE DECHERT CASE.

4

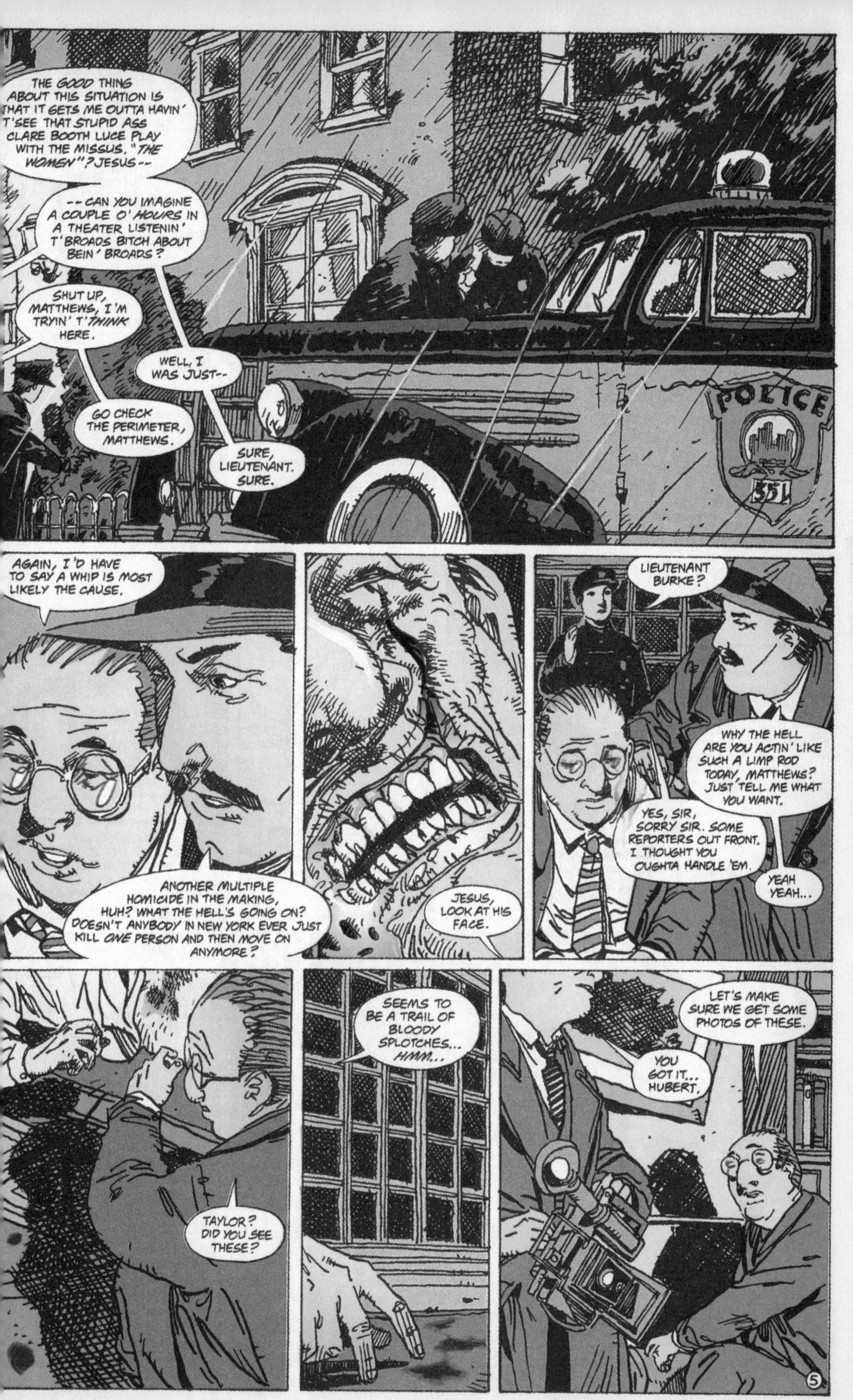
THE GOOD THING ABOUT THIS SITUATION IS THAT IT GETS ME OUTTA HAVIN' T'SEE THAT STUPID ASS CLARE BOOTH LUCE PLAY WITH THE MISSUS. "THE WOMEN"? JESUS--
--CAN YOU IMAGINE A COUPLE O' HOURS IN A THEATER LISTENIN' T'BROADS BITCH ABOUT BEIN' BROADS?
SHUT UP, MATTHEWS, I'M TRYIN' T'THINK HERE.
WELL, I WAS JUST--
GO CHECK THE PERIMETER, MATTHEWS.
SURE, LIEUTENANT. SURE.
POLICE
351
AGAIN, I'D HAVE TO SAY A WHIP IS MOST LIKELY THE CAUSE.
ANOTHER MULTIPLE HOMICIDE IN THE MAKING, HUH? WHAT THE HELL'S GOING ON? DOESN'T ANYBODY IN NEW YORK EVER JUST KILL ONE PERSON AND THEN MOVE ON ANYMORE?
JESUS, LOOK AT HIS FACE.
LIEUTENANT BURKE?
WHY THE HELL ARE YOU ACTIN' LIKE SUCH A LIMP ROD TODAY, MATTHEWS? JUST TELL ME WHAT YOU WANT.
YES, SIR, SORRY SIR. SOME REPORTERS OUT FRONT. I THOUGHT YOU OUGHTA HANDLE 'EM.
YEAH YEAH...
TAYLOR? DID YOU SEE THESE?
SEEMS TO BE A TRAIL OF BLOODY SPLOTCHES... HMM...
LET'S MAKE SURE WE GET SOME PHOTOS OF THESE.
YOU GOT IT... HUBERT.

AS A CHILD I HELD AN EXTREME AND UNWAVERING FEAR OF INSECTS.

THE FACT THAT MY FATHER'S HOUSE STOOD IN AN UPPER-CLASS NEIGHBOR-HOOD--

-- DID NOT PREVENT THE OCCASIONAL UN-INVITED SPIDER FROM DROPPING TO MY BED ON A SINGLE LUMINES-CENT STRAND JUST BEFORE I DRIFTED OFF TO SLEEP.

THE APPEARANCE OF SUCH A CREATURE WOULD DEPRIVE ME OF ANY REST.

I WOULD SIT UP, AWAKE, THE COVERS BUNCHED BENEATH MY COWERING CHIN UNTIL LONG AFTER THE BREAK OF THE SUN.

IT WAS LATER, IN COLLEGE, THAT I LEARNED THE SPIDERS WERE NOT INSECTS AT ALL, BUT RATHER, ARTHROPODS--

--THE SAME ORDER TO WHICH SCORPIONS BELONG.

-- IT IS SCORPIONS THAT HAVE KEPT ME AWAKE THIS NIGHT.

THE VOICE IN MY DREAMS IS UNCHANGED, THOUGH ITS WORDS ARE NOW FAR FROM MEDITATIVE...

"LONG HAD I STOOD IN THIS UNMOVING PLACE OF HEAT AND DRY DEATH--"

"--THE BLACK BIRDS SOARING ABOVE ME JUST AS I WISHED TO SOAR."

"TO SLAKE MY THIRST AND BREAK FREE OF MY COARSE SKIN--"

"--I DRANK DEEPLY OF THE LIQUID OF REBIRTH."

"AND YET, THOUGH I BECAME MORE LIKE YOU-- JUST LIKE YOU--"

"--YOU DESCEND UPON ME CRYING--"

"--YOU ARE NOT ONE OF US YOU ARE NOT ONE OF US YOU ARE NOT ONE OF US!"

"I DIED THAT DAY AS I DIE EACH DAY."

⑦

THERE'S A SAYING MAKING ITS WAY AROUND THE ISLAND LATELY-- "EVERY FLOOR OF A SKYSCRAPER SITS FIRMLY ON THE BACKS OF 1000 AMERICANS."

I CAN'T HELP BUT THINK OF THIS AS I RIDE THE FORTY FLOORS UP TO STEPHEN CUTLER'S OFFICE FOR YET ANOTHER INVESTMENT MEETING.

THOUGH I HAVE NO INTEREST IN HIS BUSINESS, IT DOES SEEM THE BEST WAY TO STAY CLOSE TO THE CRIMES INFLICTED ON HIS PARTNERS.

PLEASE COME RIGHT IN, MR. DODDS. WE'VE BEEN EXPECTING YOU.

I CERTAINLY HOPE SO. AFTER ALL, YOU DID CALL ME THIS MORNING AND ASK THAT I BE HERE, AS I RECALL.

NOW, WESLEY, DON'T GO GETTING YOUR FLANNELS IN A BUNCH!

WE JUST CAN'T STAND THE THOUGHT OF LETTING YOU LOSE OUT ON THE BEST INVESTMENT OF THE DECADE.

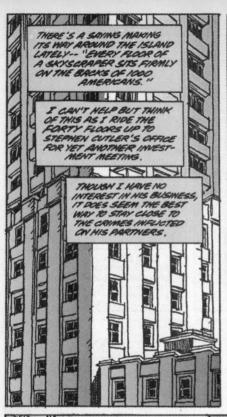

WHILE I APPRECIATE YOUR PERSISTENCE, THE MURDER OF TWO TOP OFFICIALS IN A COMPANY IS ENOUGH TO MAKE ANY POTENTIAL INVESTOR ANXIOUS, DON'T YOU THINK?

WES, YOU'RE A STRAIGHT SHOOTER, AND I LIKE THAT, BUT HEAR ME OUT.

THIS SITUATION HAS BEEN VERY DIFFICULT FOR US, BUT WE CAN'T JUST LET THIS OPPORTUNITY SLIP OUT OF OUR HANDS.

AND TO BE PERFECTLY FRANK, WITHOUT YOU WE MAY NOT BE ABLE TO SECURE THE DEAL BEFORE OTHER BACKERS SNATCH IT OUT FROM UNDER US.

SO WHAT TERRY AND I WORKED UP IS A NEW PROFIT SHARING PLAN UNDER WHICH YOU WOULD BE COMPENSATED AN EXTRA 11% ABOVE AND BEYOND WHAT YOU DISCUSSED WITH TERRY AND CASSANDRA LAST NIGHT, PLUS THE--

STEPHEN, PLEASE. I'M FLATTERED THAT YOU'D GO TO THIS MUCH TROUBLE, BUT AS I'VE ALREADY EXPLAINED, I DON'T THINK THAT EXPLOITING THE EUROPEAN WAR SITUATION TO MAKE A FAST PROFIT OFF THE OIL INDUSTRY IS ACCEPTABLE--

8

NOW, MR DODDS, DON'T *TELL* ME THAT I HAVE T'BE THE ONE T'*POINT OUT* T'YOU THAT IN BUSINESS IT'S NOT QUALITY THAT MATTERS, IT'S *QUANTITY.*

WE MAY HAVE OUR ROUGH EDGES HERE AND THERE, BUT THE BOTTOM LINE IS THAT NO OTHER INVESTMENT OPPORTUNITY IN THE CURRENT MARKETPLACE IS GOING TO BE ABLE TO PROVIDE YOU WITH THIS LEVEL OF POTENTIAL.

OH *COME* NOW, MR. STETSON, WE *BOTH* KNOW THAT QUALITY IS FAR *MORE* IMPORTANT A FACTOR. IT'S QUALITY THAT LASTS. AND WHAT LASTS PAYS OFF IN THE LONG-RUN AS *WELL* AS THE SHORT.

THIS IS 1938, MR.DODDS. THE *LONG TERM* WON'T BE VISIBLE AGAIN UNTIL THE FORTIES, *IF* THEN. AND WE'RE ONLY LOOKING FOR YOU TO INVEST FOR THE FIRST YEAR. AFTER THAT IF YOU'RE NOT HAPPY, WE'LL BUY YOU RIGHT BACK OUT.

WHAT TERRY IS TRYING TO SAY IS THAT WE ARE SO CONFIDENT THAT THIS INVESTMENT IS GOING TO PRODUCE A HIGH YIELD THAT AFTER A YEAR'S TIME YOU'LL BE BEGGING US TO LET YOU INCREASE YOUR SHARE.

CASSANDRA'S RIGHT ON IT, MR.DODDS. YOU DON'T NEED ME TO TELL YOU THAT THIS WAR'S ON ITS WAY TO AMERICA.

ANYBODY LOOKIN' AT THE WORLD KNOWS *THAT,* AND WHEN THE WAR *HITS* OUR SHORES, WHOEVER'S GOT THE OIL IS GONNA HAVE THE GOLD.

YOU...WELL,YOU *DO* HAVE A POINT THERE. I HATE THE IDEA OF MAKING MONEY OFF THE WORLD'S DILEMMAS, BUT I MUST ADMIT... YOU'VE GOT ME THINKING.

YOU'RE A SHARP ARGUER, MR. STETSON. I'M *STILL* NOT SOLD, BUT... I'LL THINK THIS OVER A LITTLE MORE.

I'LL BE IN TOUCH.

NCHK!

NICELY DONE, TERRY.

NICELY DONE.

37

BING BONG

HELLO? HUMPHRIES? ARE YOU HOME?

YES, MISS BELMONT. I'M SORRY I COULDN'T GET TO THE DOOR FASTER. IT IS A VERY LARGE HOUSE, AS YOU WELL KNOW.

NO, I'M SORRY, HUMPHRIES. I'M JUST VERY EXCITED TO GIVE WESLEY THIS GIFT I GOT HIM.

CERTAINLY. ALLOW ME TO HELP YOU WITH IT. MR. DODDS IS--

I KNOW HE'S NOT HERE, HE TOLD ME HE HAD A LUNCH MEETING THIS AFTERNOON, BUT I WAS HOPING TO LEAVE THIS FOR HIM AS A SURPRISE.

DOES THIS ITEM REQUIRE ANY PARTICULAR ROOM?

ACTUALLY, I WAS THINKING THE STUDY.

WES ALWAYS SEEMS SO RESOLUTE IN HERE. THIS MIGHT JUST BE THE THING TO LIVEN HIM UP A LITTLE.

IS THERE ANYTHING YOU WOULD LIKE ME TO TELL MR. DODDS ABOUT THE GIFT?

ALREADY TAKEN CARE OF. I HAVE A NOTE HERE IN MY CLUTCH.

AND... THE PERFECT MESSENGER.

UH, MISS BELMONT, PLEASE. THAT IS--

I KNOW. WES LOVES THIS THING. DON'T WORRY, I'LL BE CAREFUL.

I JUST WANT TO MAKE SURE HE NOTICES MY NOTE--

--AND I THINK THIS WILL BE JUST THE WAY TO ENSURE IT.

YES, QUITE.

HUMPHRIES, YOU'VE BEEN A GEM. THANK YOU EVER SO MUCH.

MY PLEASURE, MISS BELMONT, AS ALWAYS.

TA!

10

--AND I WANT PAUL AND ISABEL INVITED AS WELL. WE *STILL* DON'T HAVE ANY SOLID CONNECTIONS INTO FRANCE, AND THEY MIGHT JUST BE OUR GATE-WAY.

YES, MISS CUTLER. WILL THERE BE ANYTHING *ELSE?*

OH, THERE *ALWAYS* IS, BUT YOU CAN JUST CHECK BACK WITH ME AFTER YOU'VE GOTTEN THOSE INVITATIONS OUT.

VERY GOOD, MISS CUTLER.

WHAT'S *THIS...?*

DINNER TONIGHT?
  --T.

I SHOULD HAVE KNOWN... T AS IN *TEXAS.*

IN THE FLESH.

THE CACTUS IS VERY NICE, TERRY. WHAT A UNIQUE GIFT.

TOUGH EXTERIOR PROTECTIN' A BEAUTIFUL AND FRAGILE BLOOM SEEMED APPROPRIATE.

I DON'T KNOW WHAT TO SAY...

WELL THEN SAY YES.

YOU REALLY ARE A CONSTANT SURPRISE, BUT I SIMPLY DON'T LIKE TO GET INVOLVED WITH PEOPLE IN THE WORKPLACE.

IF WE'RE OUT AT DINNER, WE WON'T *BE* IN THE WORK-PLACE.

⑪

YOU *KNOW* WHAT I MEAN, TERRY.

CASSANDRA, YOU ARE A BEAUTIFUL WOMAN. AND THOUGH I ADMIRE YOUR WORK ETHIC, YOU STAY *HERE* EVERY NIGHT WHEN YOU *SHOULD* BE OUT ON THE TOWN *SHARING* THAT BEAUTY WITH THE REST OF MANHATTAN... OR CUTTING A RUG UP IN HARLEM.

HOW MANY WOMEN DO YOU KNOW WHO ARE IN THE POSITION *I'M* IN? I *HAVE* TO WORK TWICE AS HARD TO PROVE THAT I'M NOT JUST HERE BECAUSE I'M MY FATHER'S DAUGHTER.

THAT MAY BE TRUE, BUT YOU CERTAINLY *DON'T* HAVE TO PROVE THAT TO *ME*.

I-- OHHH... *ONE* DINNER.

BUT *ABOVE* THAT I CAN'T PROMISE YOU ANYTHING *MORE*. SHALL WE MAKE RESERVATIONS?

ALREADY MADE. A TABLE FOR TWO AT THE PERSIAN ROOM. EDDIE DUCHIN'S THERE TONIGHT. I'LL PICK YOU UP AT YOUR PLACE AT EIGHT.

"ALREADY MADE THEM"... WHAT A PUSHOVER I TURNED OUT TO BE, *HUH?*

"TOUGH EXTERIOR"... RIGHT. ALL LOOKS AND NO--

OW!

HUMPHRIES?

SOMEONE APPEARS TO HAVE BEEN IN MY STUDY--

YES, SIR. THAT WAS MISS BELMONT. I BELIEVE SHE LEFT YOU A NOTE...?

"MY DEAREST WES, FOR THE MAN WHO HAS EVERYTHING... SOMETHING NEW. I WANTED TO BE THE ONE TO BRING A LITTLE MUSIC INTO YOUR LIFE. HARMONIOUSLY YOURS, DIAN."

AH, GOOD, YOU FOUND IT. I TRIED TO TELL MISS BELMONT NOT TO--

IT'S ALL RIGHT, HUMPHRIES. YOU NEEDN'T TELL ME ABOUT DIAN'S PERSISTENCE. LET'S JUST SEE WHAT SHE'S BROUGHT US.

WELL, I'LL BE. IT'S A NEW PHONO-GRAPH PLAYER, ALONG WITH A PHONOGRAPH.

WOW! IT'S LOUIS ARMSTRONG! ISN'T IT TERRIFIC?

RCA VICTOR

TIK-- SSSHHHCRKSHHSSS

WHY YES, SIR. YOUR TEA, SIR?

I ONLY WISH I HAD THE TIME TO TAKE HER OUT AND THANK HER PROPERLY THIS EVENING.

I SEE. I TAKE IT THEN THAT YOU WILL BE HEADING OUT, HOWEVER?

YES... I'M AFRAID SO.

I CAN ONLY HOPE THAT DIAN WILL UNDERSTAND--

13

--AND THAT SOMEDAY THERE WILL BE NO NEED TO HAVE THIS FACADE SEPARATING US.

THAT SHE WILL COME TO KNOW THE IMPORTANCE OF MY SECRETS.

AND WHY SOMETIMES MY OTHER LIFE MUST TAKE PRECEDENCE OVER OUR TIME TOGETHER.

OF COURSE THE WAY THAT TECHNOLOGY IS ADVANCING, I MAY SOON BE ABLE TO DO BOTH.

--LAMBERT? THIS IS BURKE... ANY NEW LEADS ON THE WHIP KILLER AT YOUR END?

...NO, NOTHIN' CONCRETE, HERE EITHER.

KLEIN JUST SHOWED ME SOME PICS HE TOOK OF SOME MARKS ON THE FLOOR. HE'S GOT SOME THEORIES, BUT NOTHIN' WORTH REPEATIN'...

...YEAH, UH-HUM... TELL YA WHAT, MEET ME TONIGHT AROUND SIX. I THINK WE'D BETTER STAKE OUT LANG'S PLACE, IF SOMEONE'S NEXT, IT'S HIM.

TCHK

14

42

DELICIOUS AS ALWAYS, JENNY.

BETTER THAN MY MOTHER'S MATZO BALLS... ALTHOUGH I'D RATHER YOU DIDN'T TELL *HER* THAT!

"BETTER THAN MY MOTHER'S" ...WHAT WAS I *THINKING!* THAT JENNY COULD MAKE SOMEONE A VERY LUCKY MAN..

GOOD NIGHT, NOW. THE MONEY'S ON THE TABLE.

AH WELL...

CLIK

YOU!

HUBERT KLEIN. YOU ARE AN OBSERVER OF THE DEAD AND I HAVE NEED OF THEIR SECRETS.

NO, PLEASE! DON'T SHOOT ME! PLEASE--I HAVE ALLERGIES!

15

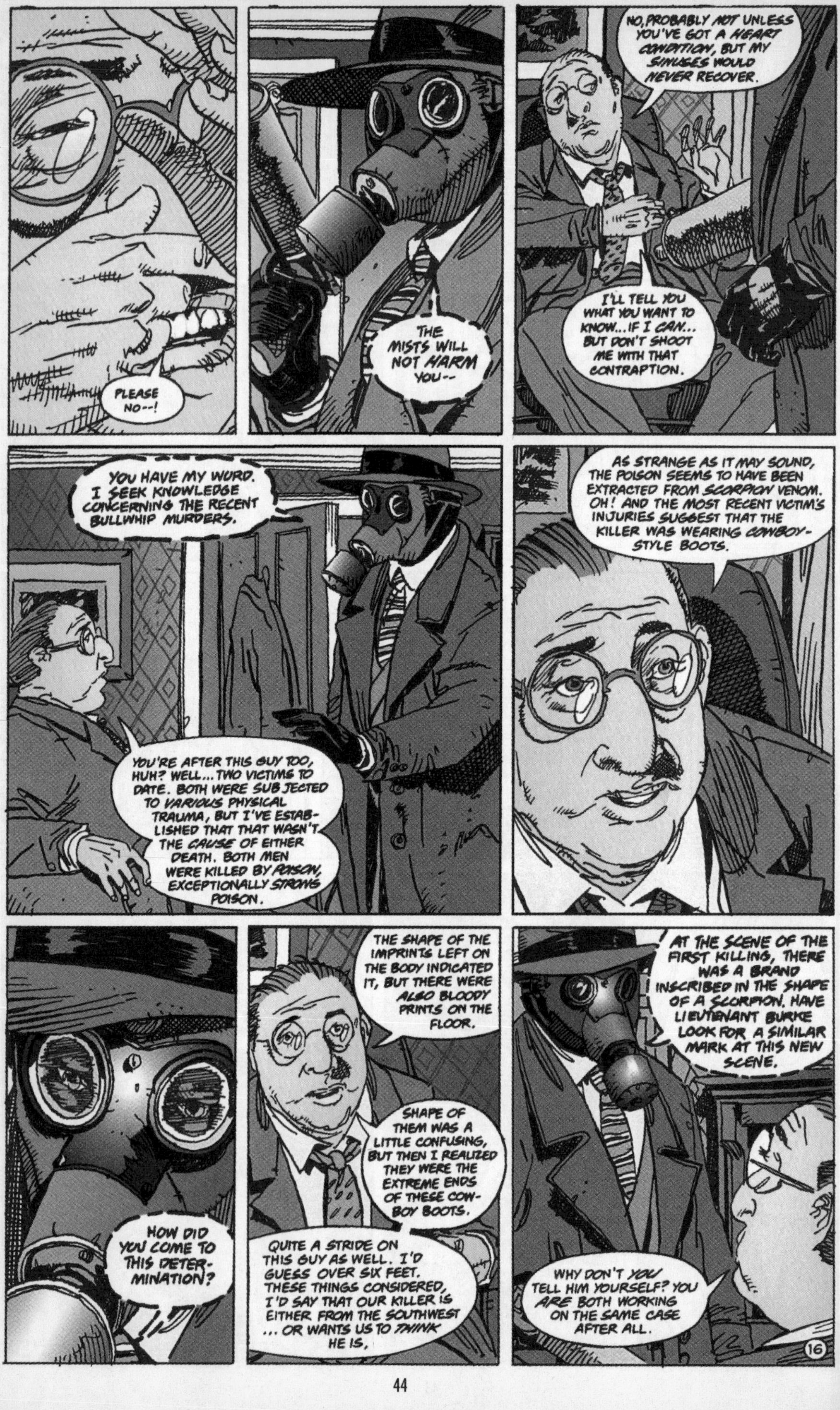
PLEASE NO--!
THE MISTS WILL NOT HARM YOU--
NO, PROBABLY NOT UNLESS YOU'VE GOT A HEART CONDITION, BUT MY SINUSES WOULD NEVER RECOVER.
I'LL TELL YOU WHAT YOU WANT TO KNOW... IF I CAN... BUT DON'T SHOOT ME WITH THAT CONTRAPTION.
YOU HAVE MY WORD. I SEEK KNOWLEDGE CONCERNING THE RECENT BULLWHIP MURDERS.
YOU'RE AFTER THIS GUY TOO, HUH? WELL... TWO VICTIMS TO DATE. BOTH WERE SUB JECTED TO VARIOUS PHYSICAL TRAUMA, BUT I'VE ESTAB-LISHED THAT THAT WASN'T THE CAUSE OF EITHER DEATH. BOTH MEN WERE KILLED BY POISON, EXCEPTIONALLY STRONG POISON.
AS STRANGE AS IT MAY SOUND, THE POISON SEEMS TO HAVE BEEN EXTRACTED FROM SCORPION VENOM. OH! AND THE MOST RECENT VICTIM'S INJURIES SUGGEST THAT THE KILLER WAS WEARING COWBOY-STYLE BOOTS.
HOW DID YOU COME TO THIS DETER-MINATION?
THE SHAPE OF THE IMPRINTS LEFT ON THE BODY INDICATED IT, BUT THERE WERE ALSO BLOODY PRINTS ON THE FLOOR.
SHAPE OF THEM WAS A LITTLE CONFUSING, BUT THEN I REALIZED THEY WERE THE EXTREME ENDS OF THESE COW-BOY BOOTS.
QUITE A STRIDE ON THIS GUY AS WELL. I'D GUESS OVER SIX FEET. THESE THINGS CONSIDERED, I'D SAY THAT OUR KILLER IS EITHER FROM THE SOUTHWEST ... OR WANTS US TO THINK HE IS.
AT THE SCENE OF THE FIRST KILLING, THERE WAS A BRAND INSCRIBED IN THE SHAPE OF A SCORPION. HAVE LIEUTENANT BURKE LOOK FOR A SIMILAR MARK AT THIS NEW SCENE.
WHY DON'T YOU TELL HIM YOURSELF? YOU ARE BOTH WORKING ON THE SAME CASE AFTER ALL.
16

THOUGH OUR GOALS ARE *INDEED* SIMILAR, LIEUTENANT BURKE AND I DO NOT SEE THE WORLD THROUGH THE SAME EYES.

SO... LET ME GET THIS STRAIGHT. YOU'RE SOME SORT OF REAL-LIFE VIGILANTE DETECTIVE? LIKE DICKIE BONES, BUT IN A GAS MASK?

WHO?

YOU KNOW... DICKIE BONES, THE PULP HERO. WAIT A MINUTE... I THINK I HAVE ONE AROUND--

--HERE--DICKIE BONES. HE'S A CHARACTER IN THESE SHOOT-EM-UP CRIME THRILLERS. IS THAT WHAT *YOU'RE* SUPPOSED TO BE? HEH!

YSTER THEATRE MAGAZINE MAY 11 10¢

DICKIE BONE

"THE DANSE MA by ALEX BURT

I SCATTER THE DARK SANDS OF OBLIVION OVER BRUTALITY AND HATE.

I PROTECT THE SLEEP OF THE JUST BY DELIVERING THE NIGHTMARES OF THE DAMNED.

DO NOT MAKE LIGHT OF MY PURPOSE, HUBERT KLEIN, FOR NONE CAN ESCAPE THE SANDMAN'S DARK DREAM.

NO! MY ALLERGIES! YOU FORGOT ABOUT MY ALLERGIES! DON'T--

SHOOT--?

"SANDMAN," HUH? OH WELL... COULDN'T *HURT.*

17

HELLO, HUMPHRIES, IT'S DIAN BELMONT CALLING. IS WES THERE?...OH... SO I TAKE IT HE HASN'T COME *BACK* YET, THEN?

OH HE *DID?*... WELL, UH, DID HE HAPPEN TO SEE MY... HE *DID*... NO, I JUST THOUGHT THAT HE WOULD CALL TO... *UH HUH*...

WELL THAT'S VERY NICE OF *YOU*, HUMPHRIES... OF COURSE IT WOULD HAVE BEEN *NICER* COMING FROM WESLEY HIMSELF, BUT THANK *YOU* AT LEAST.

OH, NO... THERE'S *NO* NEED TO TELL HIM I CALLED.

NO NEED AT ALL...

POP

CHAMPAGNE?

OF COURSE. ONLY THE BEST FOR *YOU*.

TERRY, I'M SORRY I WAS SO STAND-OFFISH EARLIER. I'VE JUST ALWAYS HAD DIFFICULTY BEING TAKEN SERIOUSLY AT WORK AND-- WELL, *YOU* KNOW HOW IT IS.

ABSOLUTELY. BUT EVEN THOUGH YOU'RE WILLING T'BE SEEN IN PUBLIC WITH A GUY LIKE ME, MY OPINION OF YOU WON'T DROP AT ALL! A TOAST--

TO?

TO POSSIBILITIES.

I'LL DRINK TO *THAT*.

DAMN BUBBLES. NEVER *HAVE* GOTTEN USED TO THIS STUFF.

16

I TAKE IT YOU WEREN'T BROUGHT UP ON CHAMPAGNE LUNCHEONS?

ME? NAH. MEN DRINK BEER OR WHISKEY IN TEXAS, NOT THIS FIZZY STUFF.

WHAT *WAS* IT LIKE GROWING UP IN THE WEST? I IMAGINE IT WAS QUITE DIFFERENT THAN MANHATTAN.

ONE MAJOR DIFFERENCE IS THAT THERE AREN'T ANY FILLIES LIKE YOURSELF DOWN SOUTH.

I'M *SERIOUS,* TERRY.

WELL, MY FATHER WAS A RAILROAD WORKER, BUT HE CAME UP WITH A NEW TYPE OF LOCKING CLAMP AND MADE A BUNDLE, SO I GOT TO BE THE FIRST STETSON TO MAKE IT TO COLLEGE, TEXAS A&M--

--GET THE HELL OUTTA M'WAY! ;HIC;

MY GOODNESS, WHAT WAS *THAT?*

MY APOLOGIES, SIR, BUT WE *DO* HAVE A DRESS CODE HERE AND YOU--

I--AM BUSTER CALHOUN, YOU COWPIE! I'M A STAR! I DRESS--DRESS LIKE THIS *WHEREVER* I GO! *INCLUDING* THIS LITTLE--POISON PIT OF YOURS.

SIR? I'M GOING TO HAVE TO ASK YOU TO--

YOU AIN'T GONNA ASK ME *NOTHIN'!* I'LL LEAVE THIS SWILL SHACK WHEN I'M ;HIC; DARN GOOD AN' READY TO! NOW YOU BETTER GET YER HANDS OFFA ME OR I'M GONNA KICK THE SHIT OUTTA *YOU!*

WHASSA MATTER? I'M NOT GOOD ENOUGH FOR YOUR--

THAT WAS CERTAINLY... COLORFUL. I'M GLAD HE DIDN'T SHOW UP TO *OUR* FUNCTION DRUNK. IS THAT A *TYPICAL* TEXAS DISPOSITION?

NO. I'M SORRY YOU HAD TO BE SUBJECTED TO THAT, CASSANDRA--

WHILE I AM PROUD OF MY HOMESTATE, THERE ARE SOME THINGS ABOUT IT THAT I'D RATHER FORGET ALTOGETHER.

⑲

--SO ANYHOW, WE CAME TO BE PRETTY WELL KNOWN AROUND TEXAS AND I THOUGHT THE TIME HAD COME TO TRY MY HAND AT A *REAL* CITY. THE REST, AS THEY SAY, IS HISTORY.

WHAT A *FASCINATING* STORY. IT MUST HAVE BEEN QUITE EXHILARATING COMING TO A NEW CITY, ALONE, AND HAVING TO START AT THE BOTTOM OF THE SOCIAL STRATA ALL OVER AGAIN. I ADMIRE THAT.

IT'S BEEN A MIGHT DIFFICULT TO MAKE THE ADJUSTMENT...BUT I *LOVE* A GOOD CHALLENGE.

I HAD A *WONDERFUL* EVENING, TERRY. WOULD YOU LIKE TO COME IN FOR A NIGHTCAP?

I'D LIKE THAT VERY MUCH.

OH-- THERE YOU TWO ARE-- WELL-- 'BOUT TIME-- S'ALMOS' *MIDNIGHT*.

FATHER? WHAT'S THE MATTER. WHY ARE YOU SITTING ALONE IN THE DARK? HAVE YOU BEEN DRINKING?

OH JUSSA BIT. NOTHIN' *MAJOR*--YET.

WHAT IS IT? WHAT'S THE MATTER?

DEAD IN TH' WATER, CASSIE. DODDS CALLED AN' DECLINED TH' INVEST- MENT. PULLED OUT. NOT EVEN A *MAYBE*.

WHAT? *WHY*, FOR GOD'S SAKE?

DON'T KNOW--

DON'T WORRY, FATHER. I'M SURE THERE'S SOMEONE ELSE WE CAN FIND TO--

FUCK THAT LITTLE FOUR-EYED MULE SUCKER!

TERRY!

NOW CALM DOWN THERE, SON. NO REASON T'FLY OFF THE HANDLE--

CASSANDRA? MR. CUTLER? I'M SORRY, BUT I'LL BE *DAMNED* IF I'M GONNA LET THIS FALL APART *NOW*. IF YOU'LL *EXCUSE* ME.

20

Baah da duh duh--

Doah da duh duh--

Baaaaaa duh!

THANK YOU! THANK YOU...

THIS CONCLUDES OUR BROADCAST OF "BELSHAZZAR'S FEAST," THE NEW WORK BY BRITISH COMPOSER WILLIAM WALTON. TONIGHT'S NEW YORK PHILHARMONIC ORCHESTRA WAS UNDER THE DIRECTION OF THE INIMITABLE TOSCANINI--

--COMING UP NEXT... THE JUPITER PLAYHOUSE AND THEIR PRODUCTION OF DEVIL MAY CARE--

MISTER LANG? YOUR WATER IS DRAWN, SIR.

AH, RUDY. DID YOU HEAR THE SYMPHONY? IT WAS QUITE CARNAL. VERY PAGAN IN ITS RHYTHMS.

QUITE UNCHARACTERISTIC FOR A WALTON PIECE. IT HAS STIRRED ME.

YES SIR?

OH, YES... QUITE.

I FOUND IT AROUSING, BUT STILL A TRIFLE... UNSATISFYING. IT LACKED A FINAL... RELEASE. I NEED THAT RELEASE, RUDY.

YOU REALLY ARE A VERY PRETTY BOY. ARE THERE ANY MORE OF YOU AT HOME?

JUST MY BROTHER, MAURICE, MR. LANE.

21

MMMMMMMM...

MAURICE, HM? WE MAY HAVE TO SEE ABOUT SECURING *HIS* SERVICES HERE AS WELL.

YEE-YIKES!

WHAT *IS* IT, LAMBERT?

ENOUGH TO MAKE A GUY SICK. HERE. LOOK FOR YOURSELF.

UH HUH. SO LANG LIKES TO GET HIS WHISTLE POLISHED BY HIS HOUSEBOY, *HUH?*

IT'S DOWNRIGHT SICK.

SO HE'S A PERVERT. SO WHAT? WE AIN'T OUT LOOKIN' TO ARREST A DEGENERATE. WE'RE HOLDIN' OUT FOR A *KILLER.*

STILL, IT'S PRETTY APPALLIN'! HM...YEP...SICK AS ALL GET OUT...

WELL, JUST KEEP WATCHIN'. DOESN'T LOOK LIKE IT'S GONNA GO DOWN TONIGHT, BUT WE'LL STAY UP A LITTLE LONGER.

YEAH, WELL, LANG WON'T... IF YOU CATCH MY DRIFT--

22

THESE NIGHTS SEEM TO GET LONGER AND LONGER.

BUT THE DREAMS, IF ANYTHING, DRIVE ME TO INCREASE MY ACTIVITIES.

CLAC

HOW LONG CAN THIS LAST?

HOW MUCH HORROR AND CRIME AND MORAL TRANSGRESSION CAN ONE CITY FIND WITHIN ITSELF?

I WONDER IF THE PULP SLEUTHS HAVE ACHING JOINTS-- NEEDLING PAINS IN THE SMALL OF THE BACK--

--VOICES IN THE BACK OF THEIR HEADS.

23

I WISH IT WEREN'T SO LATE. I'D GIVE DIAN A CALL IF THE HOUR WASN'T SO ABOMINABLE--

BUT IT'S ALWAYS LATE FOR YOU THESE DAYS, ISN'T IT, WES?

CHINK

HM--?

HUMPHRIES?

WHAT IN THE WORLD...?

MY GOD.

THAT'S A NICE DOLL BABY YOU'VE GOT THERE, LITTLE BOY--

--WHAT SAY I PUT YOU BOTH DOWN FOR SOME SHUT-EYE?

...AT THE *W.P.A.* ART SHOW, AND HE SAID HE COULDN'T AFFORD IT.

COULDN'T *AFFORD* IT? HOW DROLL...

DONG DONG

OH! HELLO, JUDGE SCHAEFFER.

GOOD AFTER-NOON, DIAN. I WAS HOPING TO HAVE A WORD WITH *YOUR* FATHER. IS HE IN?

ACTUALLY, HE *ISN'T*, BUT I EXPECT HIM BACK AT ANY TIME. IN FACT I THOUGHT *YOU* MIGHT BE HIM. PLEASE, COME IN AND WE'LL HAVE SOME COFFEE AND SEE IF HE TURNS UP.

WELL, NOW, I DON'T WANT TO *TROUBLE* YOU--

IT'S NO TROUBLE. I WAS JUST READING, BUT IT'S *CHAUCER*, SO I COULD *USE* A BREAK.

CHAUCER, EH? I HAVEN'T HEARD OF HIM SINCE MY UNIVERSITY DAYS.

YES, WELL, MY--*FRIEND*--WESLEY DODDS LENT IT TO ME, SO I--

YOU AND WESLEY, EH? I NEVER WOULD HAVE THOUGHT, OF COURSE I CAN SEE WHY HE'S ATTRACTED TO A LOVELY YOUNG WOMAN LIKE *YOURSELF*, BUT HE SEEMS A LITTLE... WELL, OVERWORKED.

I KNOW HE CAN BE A BIT DISTANT AT TIMES, BUT ACTUALLY, WES IS *VERY* FUN AND COMPASSIONATE IN HIS OWN FASHION.

IN *CERTAIN* WAYS, HE'S THE *MOST NORMAL* MAN I EVER DATED.

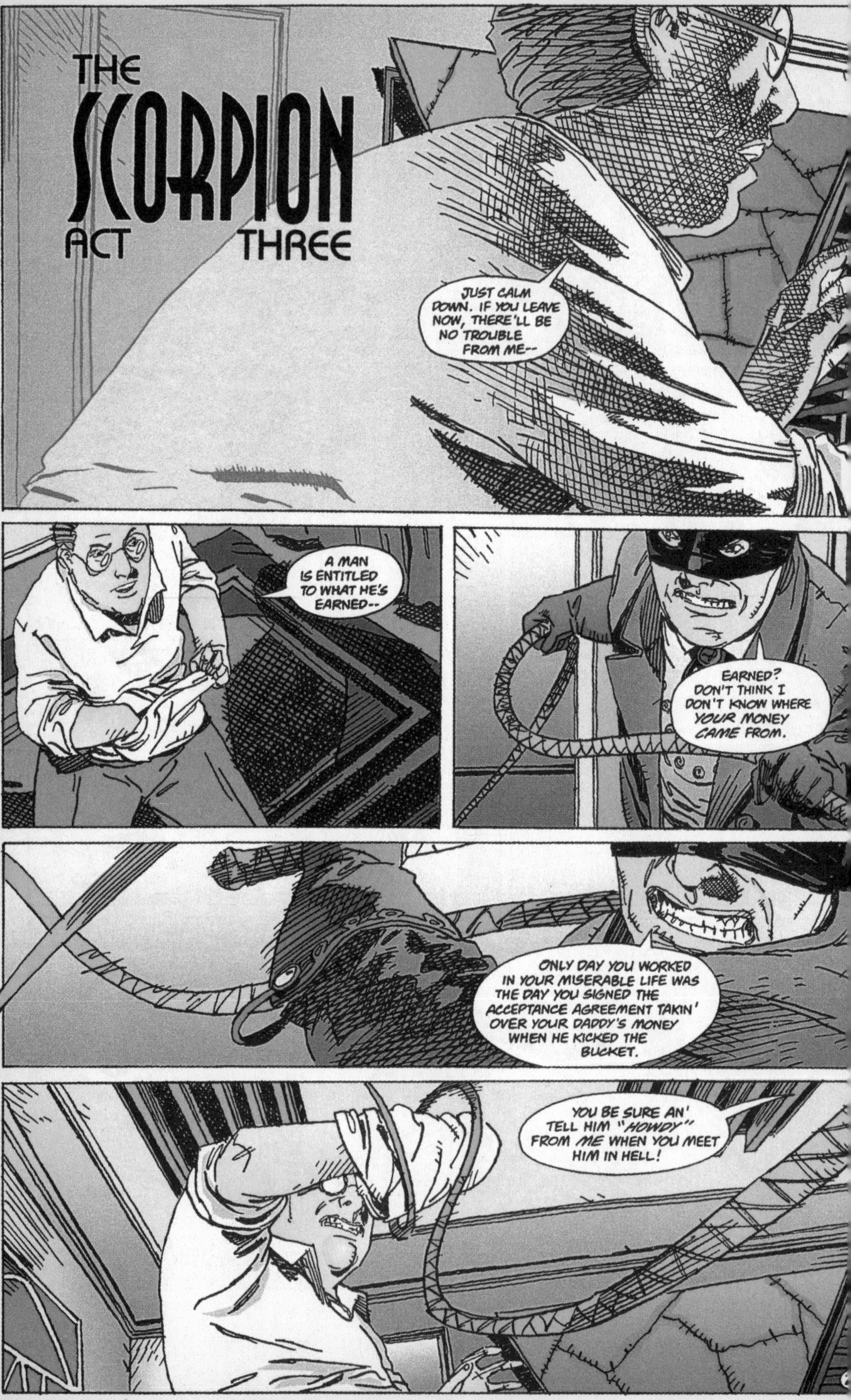
THE SCORPION
ACT THREE
JUST CALM DOWN. IF YOU LEAVE NOW, THERE'LL BE NO TROUBLE FROM ME--
A MAN IS ENTITLED TO WHAT HE'S EARNED--
EARNED? DON'T THINK I DON'T KNOW WHERE YOUR MONEY CAME FROM.
ONLY DAY YOU WORKED IN YOUR MISERABLE LIFE WAS THE DAY YOU SIGNED THE ACCEPTANCE AGREEMENT TAKIN' OVER YOUR DADDY'S MONEY WHEN HE KICKED THE BUCKET.
YOU BE SURE AN' TELL HIM "HOWDY" FROM ME WHEN YOU MEET HIM IN HELL!

YOU'RE *TYPICAL,* DODDS.

TYPICAL OF TH' WHOLE CONSPIRACY OF WEALTH THAT'S GOT A STRANGLEHOLD ON THIS COUNTRY.

TYPICAL OF EVERY RICH BASTARD WHO'S GOT MORE THAN HE COULD EVER USE BUT PLANS ON *KEEPIN'* EVERY PLUG NICKEL OF IT ANYWAY.

VERY *TRICKY,* YOU CRAFTY LITTLE BASTARD--

-- BUT IT AIN'T GONNA DO YA--HUH--?

HNH!

--WAAAAA--

--GUHFF!

YOU GODDAMN MONKEY! FIGHT LIKE A MAN, WHY DON'TCHA!

YOU MEAN LIKE ATTACKING AN UNARMED OPPONENT?

3

OH, YOU'RE ARMED. YOU'RE ARMED WITH BANK ACCOUNTS, AND TRUST FUNDS, AND DIVIDENDS--

--BUT I THINK IT'S TIME YOU GOT SOMETHING YOU CAN TRULY CALL YOUR OWN--

-- THE ONLY THING A MAN CAN EVER CALL HIS OWN--

CRAC

UNNNH!

--HIS DEATH.

NO!

NNH!

YA KNOW, DODRS, I AM KINDA SORRY ABOUT THIS--

ANNNNH! S-SORRY?

SORRY THE POISON WORKS SO FAST--

I'D A LIKED TA SEE YOU SUFFER MORE.

HUFF!

4

56

BUT YA LEARNED AN IMPORTANT LESSON HERE T'DAY, PARTNER.

YA CAN'T HAVE EVERYTHING YA WANT IN LIFE.

EVEN IF YA GOT ALL THE MONEY IN THE WORLD--

--SOMETIMES IT *STILL* AIN'T ENOUGH.

HAPPY TRAILS.

SECONDS LEFT--

--SHOULD HAVE TOLD DIAN--

--SHOULD HAVE TOLD HER--

MASTER DODDS?

--EVERY-THING...

I WAS IN THE KITCHEN AND SAW A MAN RUNNING FROM THE GROUNDS AND--

GOOD LORD!

MASTER DODDS! MASTER DODDS! OH DEAR...

5

--WE JUST HAVE TO FIND AND SECURE A NEW INVESTOR, THAT'S ALL. IN FACT I WISH TERRY WERE HERE, HE'S PROBABLY GOT SOMEONE LINED UP ALREADY.

CASSANDRA? I DON'T THINK THE PLAN HAS ANYTHING TO DO WITH THAT LONG FACE. WHAT IS IT? WHAT'S THE MATTER?

IT'S NOTHING, I--

CASSIE. I KNOW YOU WANT ME TO BE *JUST* YOUR BOSS WHEN WE'RE AT WORK, BUT AT THIS MOMENT I'M ALSO YOUR FATHER. WHAT'S WRONG? DID I UPSET YOU LAST NIGHT? IS IT *TERRY?*

IT *IS* TERRY, SOMEWHAT, BUT MOSTLY I'M WORRIED FOR *YOU.* I DON'T THINK IT'S SAFE FOR YOU TO *BE* HERE. MR. RUMMEL, AND MR. DECHERT WERE--

WERE VERY *DIFFERENT* FROM *ME.* I KNOW IT'S A TERRIBLE SITUATION, AND I'D BE LYING IF I DIDN'T SAY I WAS A *LITTLE* WORRIED, BUT WHO WOULD DARE TO ATTACK ME HERE--

MR. CUTLER? CASSANDRA? I'M SORRY TO INTRUDE, BUT I--

TERRY?

THERE YOU ARE, BOY. AFTER YOUR REACTION LAST NIGHT, WE WERE STARTING TO WONDER ABOUT YOU.

I KNOW. I REALLY FLEW OFF THE HANDLE, AND I APOLOGIZE FOR THAT. IT'S JUST THAT I'D WORKED SO *HARD* TO SECURE DODDS THAT I--

--WELL, LET'S JUST SAY THAT I GOT MYSELF TOGETHER, AND I SPOKE TO DODDS LAST NIGHT AFTER I LEFT.

I NOW REALIZE THAT HE'S A DEAD END AND THAT WE SHOULD JUST REGROUP AND TAKE A DIFFERENT TRAIL AT THIS POINT.

GLAD TO HEAR IT, SON, IN FACT I WAS *JUST* SAYING TO CASSANDRA THAT--

BZZZT

--EXCUSE ME.

YES, MRS. HOWELL?

THERE'S A LIEUTENANT BURKE TO SEE YOU, SIR, SHALL I--

DON'T WORRY, I'LL SHOW *MYSELF* IN.

AFTERNOON. YOU STEPHEN CUTLER?

UH...YES, LIEUTENANT... BURKE WAS IT?

YEAH, LOOK, SORRY TO BUST RIGHT IN BUT THIS DAY'S BEEN A REAL BALL BUSTER, IF YOU CATCH MY DRIFT--

HAVE I INTRODUCED MY DAUGHTER, CASSANDRA?

OH. SORRY. PLEASURE.

LISTEN, I'M ON THE MURDER CASE INVOLVIN' YOUR PARTNERS, AND I'VE GOT A FEW QUESTIONS. CAN WE TALK PRIVATE SOME-WHERE?

NO NEED FOR PRIVACY. CASSANDRA AND YOUNG TERRY HERE ARE FULLY AWARE OF THE SITUATION. MAYBE THEY CAN HELP SHED SOME LIGHT ON THESE TRAGIC EVENTS.

FINE. THE KILLER SEEMS TO BE SOME KIND OF WESTERN CHARACTER. NOW, THE WAY I UNDERSTAND IT, YOUR COMPANY HAS CONNECTIONS WITH A FEW TEXAS OIL FIELDS.

CAN YOU THINK OF ANYONE WHO MIGHT BE TICKED OFF WITH YOU IN THAT PART OF THE COUNTRY?

YOU MEAN ASIDE FROM THE INDIANS?

YEAH. FUNNY. THANKS.

WE'VE BEEN IN THE TEXAS OIL GAME FOR ALMOST TWENTY YEARS NOW, LIEUTENANT. IN FACT, TERRY HERE CAME TO US FROM ONE OF OUR ABERDEEN AFFILIATES.

I CAN'T REMEMBER A SINGLE INCIDENT THAT WOULD WARRANT THIS SORT OF VICIOUS ATTACK.

WELL, IF YOU DO REMEMBER SOMETHING, MAKE SURE YOU GET HOLD OF ME. NOW THE OTHER THING IS--

--WE FOUND THIS MARK AT THE SCENE OF THE CRIME.

MEAN ANYTHING TO ANYONE HERE?

CAN'T SAY I'VE EVER SEEN THAT MARK BEFORE. HOW STRANGE.

7

WHAT ABOUT YOU? GOT ANY JOKES ABOUT THIS?

IT'S A DEADLY CREATURE, MR. BURKE. NOTHING TO JOKE ABOUT.

GOT THAT RIGHT. I DON'T MEAN TO SCARE YOU FOLKS, BUT I'D KEEP A LOW PROFILE UNTIL WE CATCH THIS CREEP.

THANKS FOR YOUR TIME. I'VE GOT A FEW MORE LEADS TO FOLLOW UP, SO I'M GONNA GET GOING. YOU THINK OF ANYTHING, CONTACT THE STATION.

WE WILL, LIEUTENANT.

AFTERNOON, MR. CUTLER, MISS CUTLER--

SEE YA' ROUND, TEX.

WHAT A CHARACTER! WOULDN'T YOU SAY SO, TERRY?

TERRY?

FOR THE FIRST TIME IN AGES I AWAKE FROM A SOUND SLEEP.

OF COURSE, A POISON INDUCED COMA IS NOT THE BEST WAY TO ARRIVE AT SUCH REST--

THANKFULLY, MY ANTIDOTE MADE IT A TEMPORARY SLUMBER.

I DON'T THINK HE'S--

WESLEY? WHAT ON EARTH HAPPENED TO YOU?

OH, DIAN. HI. YOU LOOK NICE. IT'S NOTHING--

NOTHING? LOOK AT YOU! WHAT HAPPENED?

WELL, IT'S A BIT EMBARRASSING, ACTUALLY--

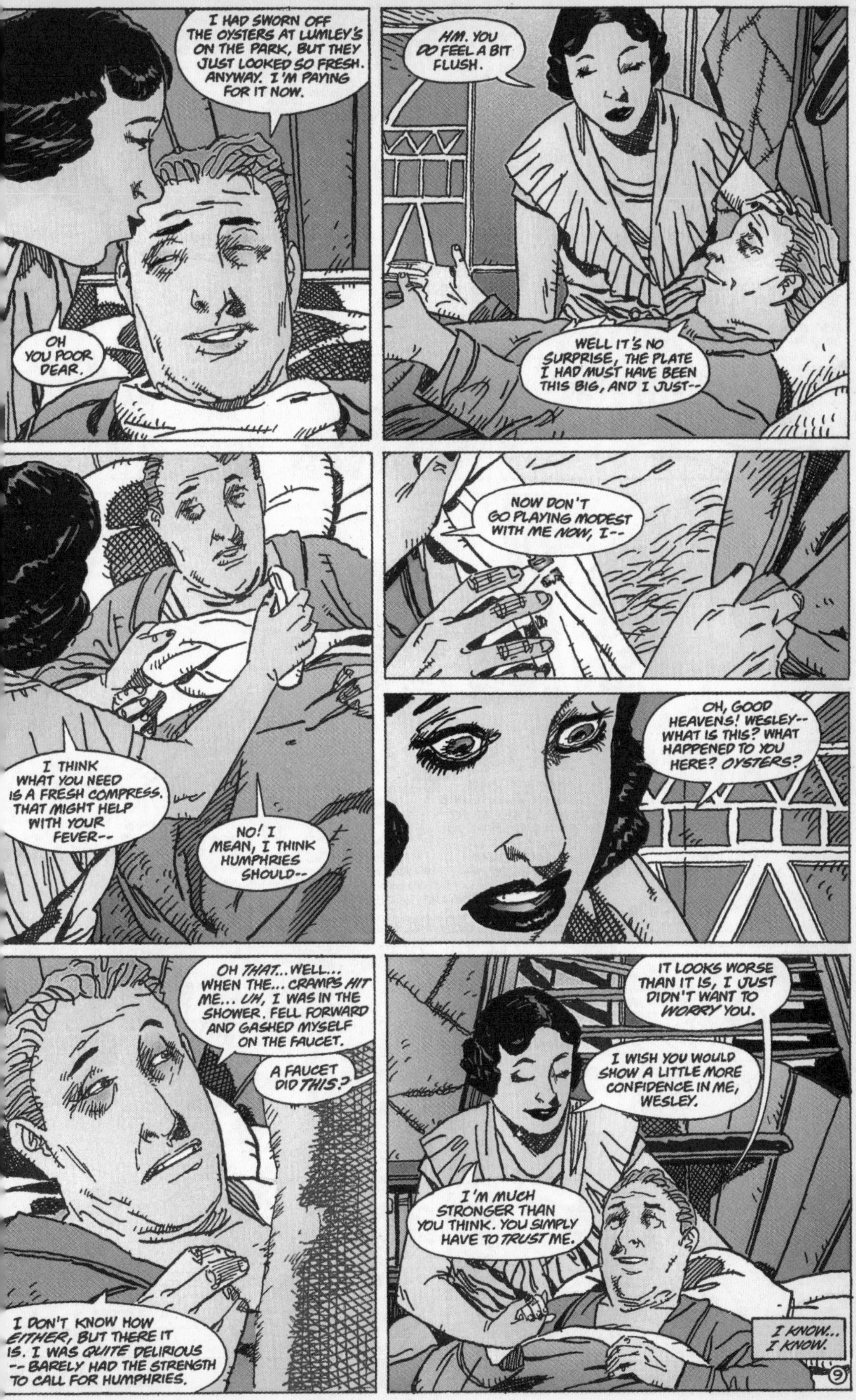
I HAD SWORN OFF THE OYSTERS AT LUMLEY'S ON THE PARK, BUT THEY JUST LOOKED SO FRESH. ANYWAY. I'M PAYING FOR IT NOW.
OH YOU POOR DEAR.
HM. YOU DO FEEL A BIT FLUSH.
WELL IT'S NO SURPRISE, THE PLATE I HAD MUST HAVE BEEN THIS BIG, AND I JUST--
I THINK WHAT YOU NEED IS A FRESH COMPRESS. THAT MIGHT HELP WITH YOUR FEVER--
NO! I MEAN, I THINK HUMPHRIES SHOULD--
NOW DON'T GO PLAYING MODEST WITH ME NOW, I--
OH, GOOD HEAVENS! WESLEY-- WHAT IS THIS? WHAT HAPPENED TO YOU HERE? OYSTERS?
OH THAT... WELL... WHEN THE... CRAMPS HIT ME... UH, I WAS IN THE SHOWER. FELL FORWARD AND GASHED MYSELF ON THE FAUCET.
A FAUCET DID THIS?
I DON'T KNOW HOW EITHER, BUT THERE IT IS. I WAS QUITE DELIRIOUS -- BARELY HAD THE STRENGTH TO CALL FOR HUMPHRIES.
IT LOOKS WORSE THAN IT IS, I JUST DIDN'T WANT TO WORRY YOU.
I WISH YOU WOULD SHOW A LITTLE MORE CONFIDENCE IN ME, WESLEY.
I'M MUCH STRONGER THAN YOU THINK. YOU SIMPLY HAVE TO TRUST ME.
I KNOW... I KNOW.
9

WHAT YOU NEED IS SOME FRESH AIR IN HERE. IT'S A BEAUTIFUL DAY OUT, AND THIS PLACE IS AS CLOSE AS A TOMB. MAY I?

YES, CERTAINLY.

HMMM. WES? WHO OWNED THIS HOUSE BEFORE YOU?

UH... A BANKER. MENDELBAUM WAS THE NAME. WHY?

I THINK HE HAD SOME STRANGE TASTES. HE APPEARS TO HAVE BRANDED THE WINDOW.

YES... WELL, I DID DO A LOT OF REDECORATING. MUST HAVE MISSED THAT.

LISTEN, I HAVE A LIBRARY VOLUNTEERS MEETING TO GET TO SO I'M GOING TO LEAVE YOU TO YOUR REST. I'LL CALL LATER TO SEE HOW YOU'RE DOING.

IN THE MEANTIME, STAY AWAY FROM THE OYSTERS.

I HAD ALWAYS HEARD THEY HAD A TOTALLY DIFFERENT EFFECT ON A MAN.

YOU JUST GET BETTER... AND WE WON'T NEED ANY OYSTERS.

OH, REALLY?

SWEET DREAMS!

I ENJOY DIAN'S BOLDNESS MORE AND MORE--

10

-- YOU LOOK LIKE YOU'RE OFF TO THE RACES.

NO, I'M JUST *BUSY*. WE STILL HAVE A BUSINESS TO ATTEND TO EVEN IN THE FACE OF THESE TERRIBLE EVENTS.

HER ABILITY TO BE PLAYFUL WITHOUT BEING VULGAR IS ENOUGH TO LIFT ANY MAN'S... SPIRITS.

WELL, I CAN *APPRECIATE* THE INITIATIVE, BUT A LADY'S GOT TO EAT, DON'T YOU THINK?

NO, I REALLY CAN'T RIGHT NOW, I--

YES, MILLIE?

BZZT

I FORGOT TO TELL YOU, MISS CUTLER. MR. WESLEY DODDS ALSO CALLED FOR YOU WHILE YOU WERE IN WITH YOUR FATHER.

THANKS, MILLIE.

DODDS? THAT'S... UNEXPECTED.

TRUE, BUT MAYBE HE'S HAD A CHANGE OF HEART.

I'D BETTER PHONE HIM RIGHT AWAY.

YES... THAT *WOULD* BE A GOOD IDEA. STRIKE WHILE THE IRON'S HOT... SO TO SPEAK.

EXACTLY.

HELLO? IS MR. DODDS THERE?... IT IS? HELLO, THIS IS CASSANDRA CUTLER RETURNING YOUR CALL...?

11

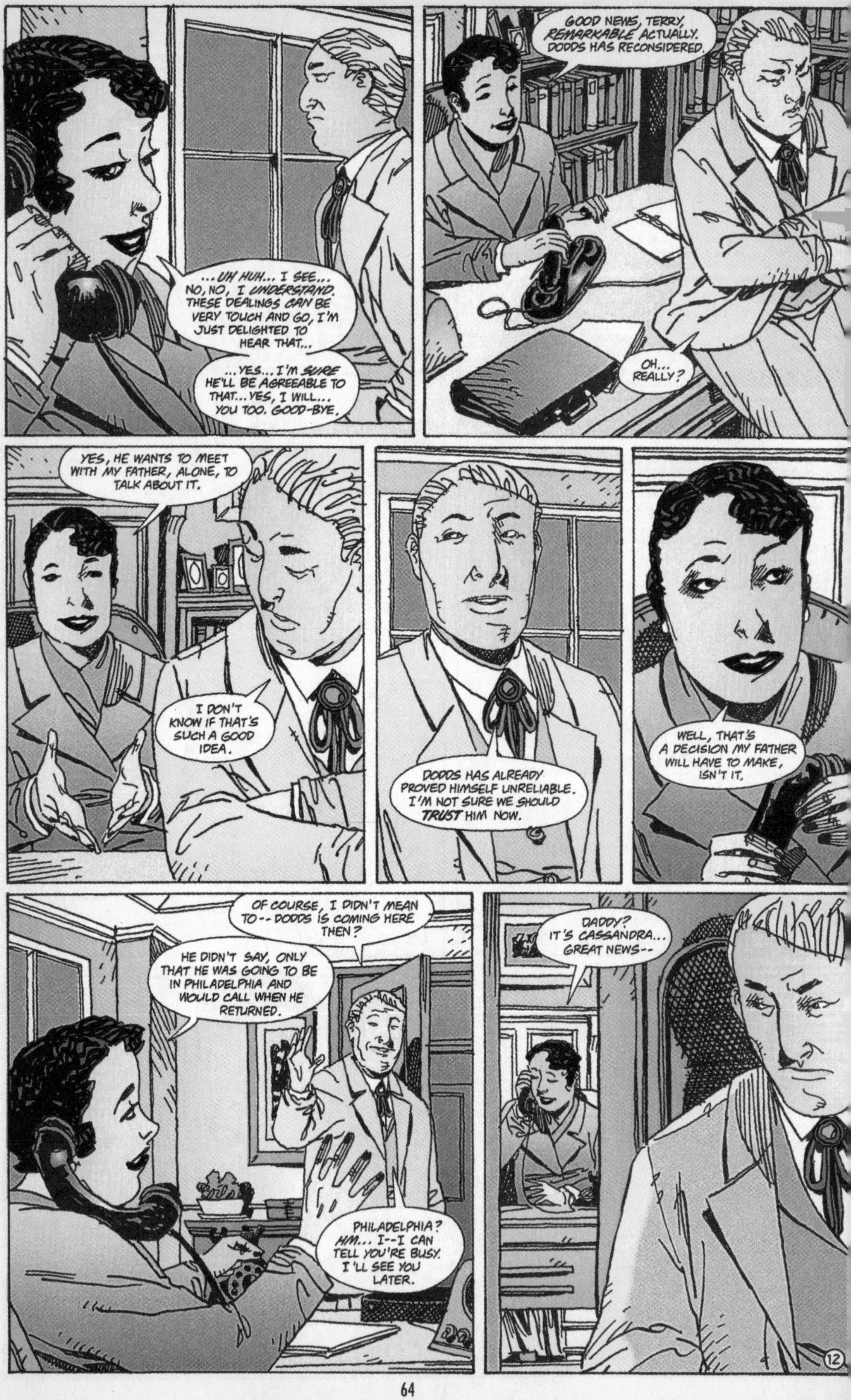
...UH HUH... I SEE... NO, NO, I UNDERSTAND. THESE DEALINGS CAN BE VERY TOUCH AND GO, I'M JUST DELIGHTED TO HEAR THAT...
...YES... I'M SURE HE'LL BE AGREEABLE TO THAT... YES, I WILL... YOU TOO. GOOD-BYE.
GOOD NEWS, TERRY, REMARKABLE ACTUALLY. DODDS HAS RECONSIDERED.
OH... REALLY?
YES, HE WANTS TO MEET WITH MY FATHER, ALONE, TO TALK ABOUT IT.
I DON'T KNOW IF THAT'S SUCH A GOOD IDEA.
DODDS HAS ALREADY PROVED HIMSELF UNRELIABLE. I'M NOT SURE WE SHOULD TRUST HIM NOW.
WELL, THAT'S A DECISION MY FATHER WILL HAVE TO MAKE, ISN'T IT.
OF COURSE, I DIDN'T MEAN TO -- DODDS IS COMING HERE THEN?
HE DIDN'T SAY, ONLY THAT HE WAS GOING TO BE IN PHILADELPHIA AND WOULD CALL WHEN HE RETURNED.
PHILADELPHIA? HM... I--I CAN TELL YOU'RE BUSY. I'LL SEE YOU LATER.
DADDY? IT'S CASSANDRA... GREAT NEWS--
12

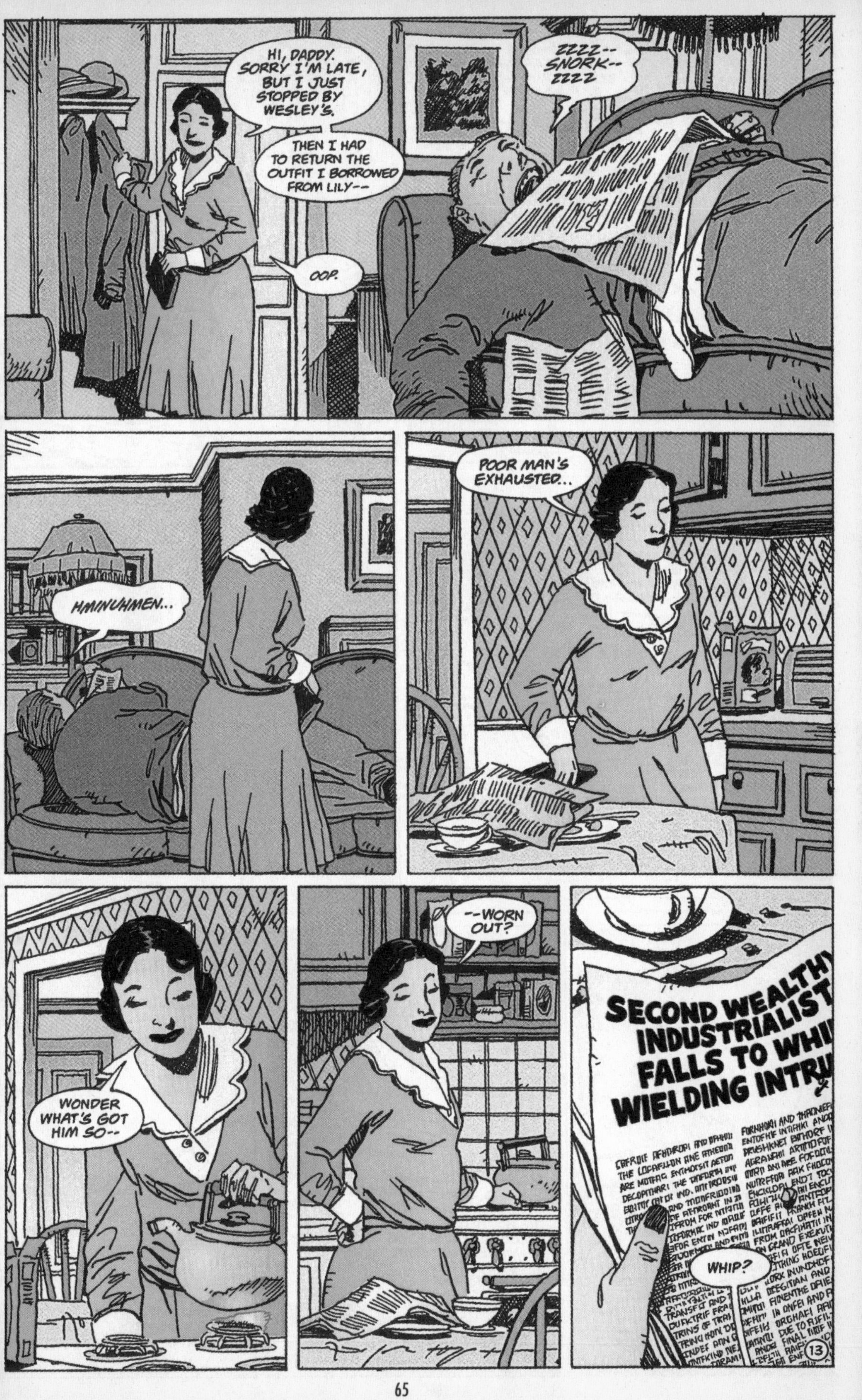
HI, DADDY. SORRY I'M LATE, BUT I JUST STOPPED BY WESLEY'S.
THEN I HAD TO RETURN THE OUTFIT I BORROWED FROM LILY--
ZZZZ-- SNORK-- ZZZZ
OOP.
HMMNUHMEN...
POOR MAN'S EXHAUSTED...
WONDER WHAT'S GOT HIM SO--
--WORN OUT?
SECOND WEALTHY INDUSTRIALIST FALLS TO WHI WIELDING INTRU
WHIP?
13

"...BOTH VICTIMS HAD LONG LASH MARKS BELIEVED TO BE CAUSED BY A BULL WHIP..."

"...RUMMEL AND DECHERT BOTH CONSIDERED AMONG MANHATTAN'S WEALTHIEST MEN..."

WHEEEEEE...

TEA TIME, SWEETHEART?

SORRY, DADDY, I SHOULD HAVE CAUGHT IT SOONER. I DIDN'T MEAN TO WAKE YOU--

'S OKAY. I WASN'T SLEEPING, I WAS JUST... RESTING MY EYES.

ACTUALLY, I WASN'T PAYING ATTENTION BECAUSE I WAS ENGROSSED IN THIS *NEWSPAPER* STORY.

I HAD NO IDEA THOSE MEN WE MET AT THE BUSTER CALHOUN SHOW HAD BEEN *KILLED.*

WHEN DID *THIS* ALL START?

THIS'S THE FIRST YOU'VE HEARD OF THAT? I'M SURPRISED.

YES, WELL, I *HAVE* HAD MY HEAD UP IN THE CLOUDS LATELY.

YAAAAWN... UMN. THAT'S WHAT'S BEEN KEEPING ME UP NIGHTS LATELY. RUMMEL AND DECHERT WERE BIG MEN IN THIS CITY.

PRESSURE'S REALLY ON TO CATCH THEIR KILLER.

CALHOUN...*HIM,* HADN'T THOUGHT OF *THAT*

ANY IDEAS YET?

OH, A FEW. HOMICIDE'S HANDLING THE FOOTWORK, OF COURSE. LOOKS TO BE A VENDETTA OF SOME SORT. STRANGE ONE TOO.

KILLER LASHES THE VICTIMS WITH A POISON-TIPPED WHIP AND THEN BRANDS A SYMBOL SOMEWHERE AT THE SCENE. THE BOYS'VE TAKEN TO CALLING HIM THE SCORPION.

DID YOU SAY... "*SCORPION*"?

(14)

...POISON-TIPPED WHIP. JESUS H. CHRIST. HASN'T THIS LUNATIC EVER HEARD OF A GUN?

ROOM SERVICE.

WHAT'S SHAKIN', SHEPARD? THE KING OF THE LUSH LIFE SPILLED IT YET?

UH, NOTHIN' SO FAH, LOOTENANT--

ACTUALLY, I MAY HAVE SOMETHIN' FOR YOU HERE, SIR.

YEAH? WHAT IS IT, CARLSON?

BUSTER CALHOUN JUST CALLED LANE AT HOME. HE'S DRUNK AS A SKUNK AND--WELL, JUST LISTEN--

I WILL IF YOU GIVE ME THE DAMNED HEADSET.

...STILL OWE ME FOR MAH SHOW! NOW, YOU'RE GONNA PAY ME TODAY OR I'M GONNA MAKE YOU WISH YOU HAD, YOU SHIT-LICKIN'--

MAN'S A REGULAR SHAKESPEARE.

LOOKS LIKE WE'VE GOT OUR TEXAN, HUH, LIEUTENANT?

WE'LL SEE. KEEP LISTENIN' AND CALL O'DONALD. TELL 'IM I'M GONNA PUT A TAIL ON CALHOUN FOR A BIT, MAYBE WE'LL GET LUCKY.

15

HUMPHRIES? THIS IS DIAN BELMONT CALLING. IS WESLEY AWAKE BY CHANCE?

I'M SORRY, MISS BELMONT, HE'S NOT. HE TOOK A SEDATIVE AND IS FAST ASLEEP.

INDEED I WILL. A GOOD EVENING TO YOU.

OH. I KNOW THIS MAY SOUND STRANGE, BUT I'M VERY WORRIED ABOUT HIM. COULD YOU LOOK IN ON HIM FAIRLY REGULARLY THIS EVENING?

OYSTERS AND FAUCETS INDEED.

--JUST VERY IMPORTANT THAT WE LET *HIM* WALK INTO THIS. I THINK TERRY HAD GOOD *INTENTIONS*, BUT HE SIMPLY PUSHED TOO HARD.

I SUPPOSE WE MIGHT *HAVE* SOUNDED A LITTLE DESPERATE TO DODDS.

I'LL CERTAINLY REMAIN SENSITIVE TO THAT APPEARANCE, CASSIE, BUT I STILL WANT ALL OF THE REPORTS AND ESTIMATES DELIVERED TO WHEREVER WE END UP MEETING JUST IN CASE.

I'LL PUT MILLIE ON THAT.

OH, BY THE BY, TERRY ASKED ME WHERE THE MEETING WAS GOING TO *BE*. HE'S THINKING OF STOPPING BY, I GUESS, SO WHEN WE FIND OUT, WE NEED TO MAKE SURE HE KNOWS.

THAT'S FUNNY. TERRY WAS IN MY OFFICE WHEN I SPOKE WITH DODDS AND HE *KNOWS* THAT DODDS REQUESTED A *PRIVATE* MEETING, JUST YOU AND HE.

THAT'S WHY I HIRED HIM! WHAT A FIREBALL THAT BOY IS.

I SUPPOSE...

16

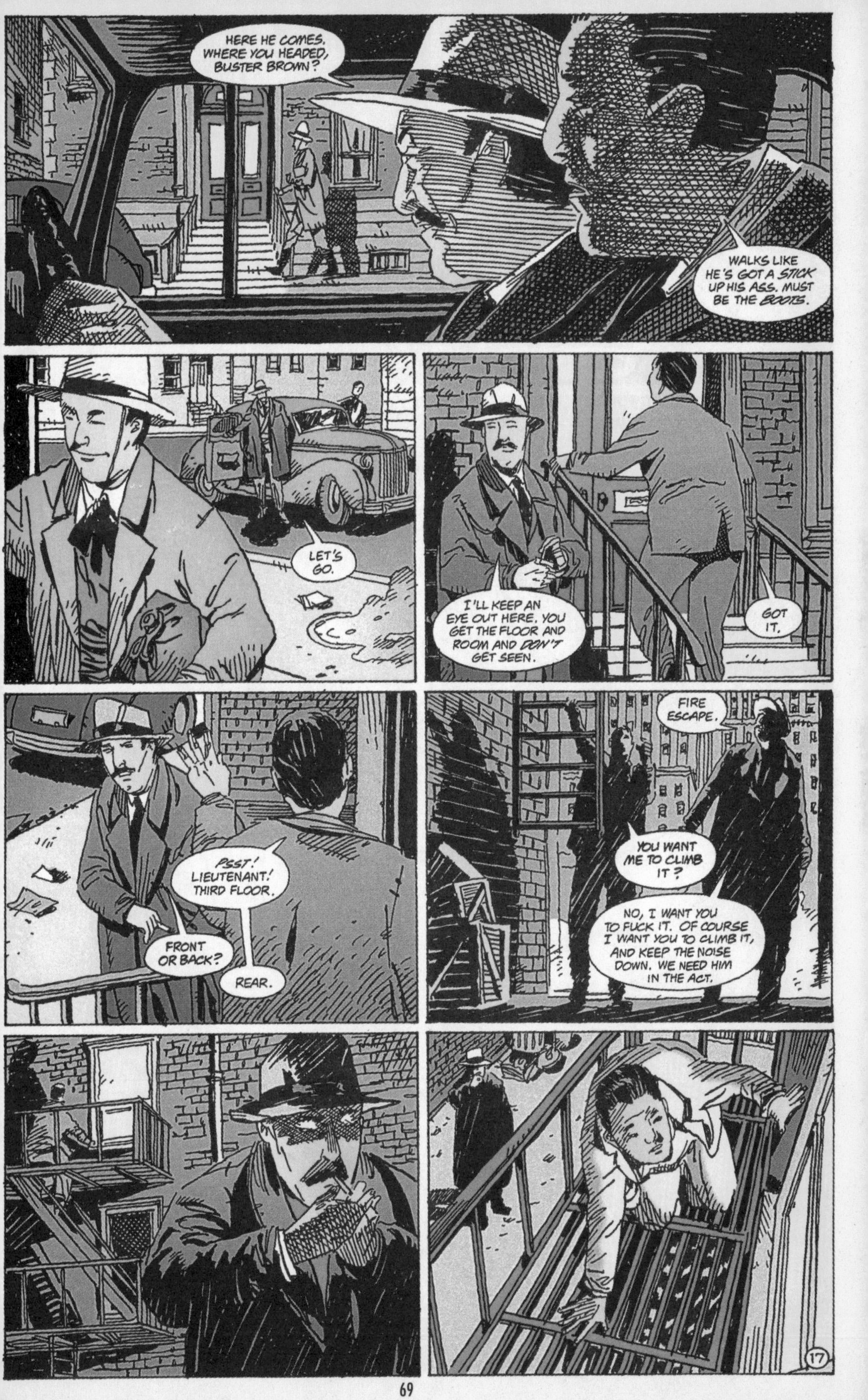
HERE HE COMES. WHERE YOU HEADED, BUSTER BROWN?
WALKS LIKE HE'S GOT A STICK UP HIS ASS. MUST BE THE BOOTS.
LET'S GO.
I'LL KEEP AN EYE OUT HERE. YOU GET THE FLOOR AND ROOM AND DON'T GET SEEN.
GOT IT.
PSST! LIEUTENANT! THIRD FLOOR.
FRONT OR BACK?
REAR.
FIRE ESCAPE.
YOU WANT ME TO CLIMB IT?
NO, I WANT YOU TO FUCK IT. OF COURSE I WANT YOU TO CLIMB IT, AND KEEP THE NOISE DOWN. WE NEED HIM IN THE ACT.
17

YOU READY TO TAKE YOUR LASHES? HUH?

EEEEEEEK!

CRAG

OMIGOD--

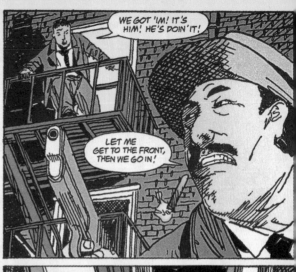

WE GOT 'IM! IT'S HIM! HE'S DOIN' IT!

LET ME GET TO THE FRONT, THEN WE GO IN!

SLAM

SLAM

THIRD FLOOR--HUFF-- REAR--HUFF--

CAN'T--HUFF-- WAIT FOR MY GODDAM-- HUFF--RETIREMENT--

WHAM

HUNH!

18

70

FREEZE, ASSHOLE! HANDS UP AND DON'T EVEN *THINK* ABOUT--

--MOVIN'--?

WHOA THERE, BUDDY! I--I--

HE AIN'T EVEN *PAID* ME FOR THIS ONE YET, SO DON'T YOU GO 'BOUT RUNNIN' ME IN.

DONE *BEEN* IN TWICE THIS WEEK AS IS.

WHAT THE HELL IS GOING ON *HERE?*

LIKE TO *RIDE* YOUR WHORES LIKE YOUR HORSES, HUH, BUSTER?

NOW, I *RESENT* THAT REMARK AND I--I--

BURKE!

WHERE THE HELL WERE *YOU?*

THE WINDOW WAS STUCK--

WHY THE HELL DIDN'T YA *BREAK* IT?

I DIDN'T WANNA *CUT* MYSELF.

OH *CHRIST.*

19

71

NO LUCK? I THOUGHT YOU HAD HIM.

YEAH, SO DID *I.* BUT HE AIN'T THE SCORPION. HE'S GOT SOME *VICES,* BUT IT DOESN'T LOOK LIKE MURDER'S ONE OF 'EM--

MY INTENTIONAL CONTACT WITH CUTLER WILL, I'M SURE, TRIGGER SUSPICION IN THE SCORPION WHO NO DOUBT BELIEVES ME DEAD.

NOW, ABOUT THIS DOE-EYED DOUCHE BAG OF A DETECTIVE YOU SENT WITH ME--

I ALLOW MYSELF TO GET LOST IN THE SWIRL OF INFORMATION AND POSSIBLE LEADS.

ALWAYS CAREFUL NOT TO PERMIT MYSELF TOO MUCH TIME TO THINK OF WHY I LOOKED DIAN STRAIGHT IN THE FACE--

--AND CONCOCTED YET ANOTHER FANTASTIC LIE TO KEEP MY TRUE SELF FROM HER.

I AM DISGUSTED IN MANY WAYS THAT I COULD MAINTAIN SUCH SECRECY.

WHY AM I SO COMFORTABLE BEING INTIMATE WITH DIAN IN EVERY WAY BUT ONE... HONESTY.

THIS CONFLICT IS TEARING AT ME, AND I KNOW I MUST SOON RESOLVE IT--

--EVEN IF IT MEANS THAT I MUST ALSO RISK LOSING HER FOREVER.

20

GOOD MORNING, TERRY.

CASSANDRA. YOU'RE MAKING AN EARLY DAY OF IT.

I JUST WANTED TO MAKE SURE I HAD A CHANCE TO TOUCH BASE WITH MY FATHER BEFORE HE--

SORRY TO SAY IT, BUT YOU'RE TOO LATE. HE STEPPED OUT A WHILE AGO TO MEET WITH LANG. PROBABLY TO DISCUSS DODDS, I'D IMAGINE.

REALLY? THEN WHAT WERE YOU DOING IN HIS OFFICE?

OH, I WAS JUST... DROPPING OFF A BUDGET REDRAFT. WANT US TO BE READY TO MOVE WHEN DODDS RECONSIDERS AT THAT MEETING TONIGHT.

YOU KNOW, TERRY, IT JUST SO HAPPENS THAT I'M FREE TONIGHT... GIVE YOU ANY IDEAS?

WELL NOW, YOU ARE A HEART-BREAKER. TURNS OUT I'M ALREADY COMMITTED FOR TONIGHT, BUT MAYBE TOMORROW--

I'D SAY THAT MAKES YOU THE HEARTBREAKER, BUT TOMORROW IT IS. I'LL BE LOOKING FORWARD TO IT--

--TEX.

21

MILLIE, I WANT YOU TO--

--I'M SORRY, I THOUGHT YOU WERE MY SECRETARY, MISS--?

DIAN. DIAN BELMONT. SORRY TO LET MYSELF IN, MISS CUTLER, BUT WE HAVE MET. THE BUSTER CALHOUN SHOW?

OH YES, OF COURSE. AND OUR *DINNER* THE OTHER EVENING. I'M SORRY I DIDN'T PLACE YOU SOONER. AND YOU'RE HERE TODAY IN REGARD TO...?

WELL, AS YOU KNOW, MY FATHER IS THE DISTRICT ATTORNEY, AND I'M HERE IN CONJUNCTION WITH HIS INVESTIGATION INTO... WELL--

THE MURDERS.

YES, EXACTLY. IT SEEMS THE DEATHS ARE ALL CENTRAL TO THE COMPANY.

CAN YOU THINK OF ANY EMPLOYEES THAT MIGHT-- UH, THAT MY FATHER MIGHT QUESTION IN THIS CASE?

MISS BELMONT, I DON'T MEAN TO BE *RUDE*, BUT ISN'T THIS A BIT UNORTHODOX? THE DISTRICT ATTORNEY SENDING HIS DAUGHTER OUT TO ROUND UP SUSPECTS?

I SIMPLY HAVE TO ASK YOU, ARE YOU HERE IN AN OFFICIAL CAPACITY?

WELL... I UNDERSTAND YOUR TREPIDATION, BUT YOU DON'T THINK I'D BE HERE IF IT *WASN'T*, DO YOU? I MEAN, EVEN *I* KNOW THAT'S *HARDLY* MY PLACE.

I... SUPPOSE. LOOK I'M SORRY I *SNAPPED* AT YOU. IT'S JUST THAT THINGS HAVE BEEN TROUBLING ME TODAY-- I MEAN-- LATELY.

IF YOU'D LIKE TO TALK ABOUT IT, I'M ALWAYS WILLING TO--

MISS BELMONT, I REALLY CAN'T JEOPARDIZE MY POSITION HERE BY SPREADING SPECULATION, BUT I WILL SAY *THIS*, I DO *THINK* THERE IS ENOUGH CAUSE TO INVESTIGATE OUR EMPLOYEES IN THIS MATTER.

THAT'S REALLY *ALL* I CAN SAY.

I UNDERSTAND. THANK YOU FOR YOUR TIME, AND IF YOU EVER JUST WANT TO TALK, CALL ME.

GOOD AFTERNOON, MISS BELMONT.

22

I'M SUPPOSED TO MEET A DRIVER NAMED HUMPHRIES. THAT YOU?

INDEED IT IS, MR. CUTLER. RIGHT THIS WAY, SIR.

UH, NOT THAT I DON'T *TRUST* YOU, MR. HUMPHRIES, BUT WHERE *IS* DODDS?

MR. DODDS HAD PLANNED TO RIDE ALONG WITH YOU, BUT HAS HAD A LAST-MINUTE CHANGE OF PLANS. HE'LL BE *MEETING* YOU AT THE HOTEL.

I ASSURE YOU THERE IS NO CAUSE FOR *ALARM.*

I'M THAT OBVIOUS, HUH? WELL, NO OFFENSE INTENDED, BUT WITH ALL OF THESE KILLINGS, ANYTHING EVEN SLIGHTLY OUTSIDE THE USUAL CAN MAKE A MAN NERVOUS.

I MEAN, FOR ALL *I* KNOW, *DODDS* COULD BE THE KILLER.

OH, I ASSURE YOU, MR. CUTLER. THERE IS *NO* POSSIBILITY OF *THAT.*

IN FACT, SECURITY IS THE PRIME REASON HE SUGGESTED HOLDING THIS MEETING SOMEWHERE OTHER THAN EXPECTED.

WELL, THAT MAKES SENSE, I SUPPOSE.

MR. DODDS ASKED ME TO GIVE YOU THIS KEY. IT IS FOR THE *LARGO* SUITE, WHERE HE WILL EITHER BE WAITING FOR YOU, OR WILL MEET YOU SHORTLY. GOOD DAY, SIR.

I CERTAINLY *HOPE* IT'S A "*GOOD DAY.*"

SLATE

HELLO?

FWIP

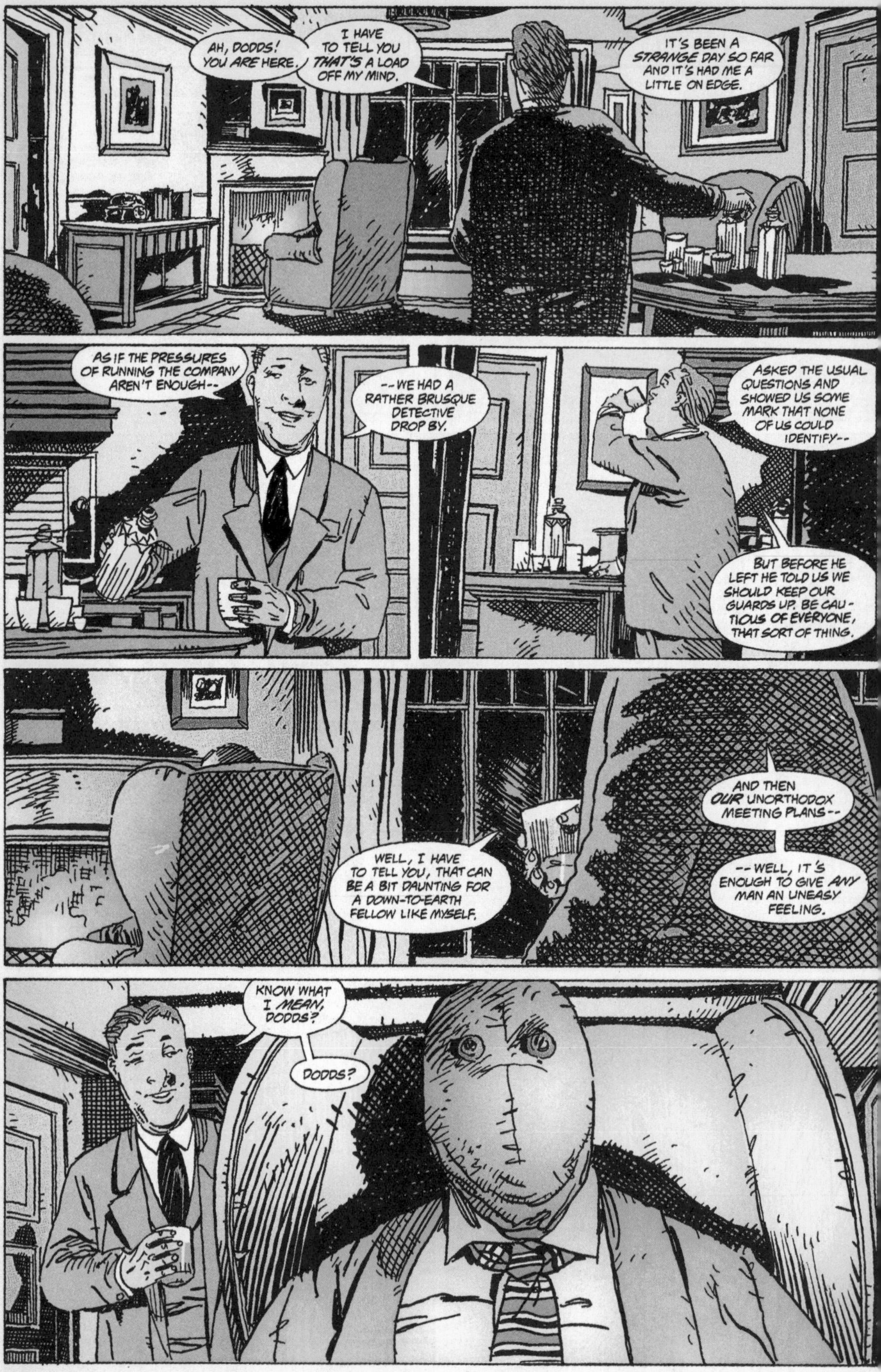
AH, DODDS! YOU ARE HERE.
I HAVE TO TELL YOU THAT'S A LOAD OFF MY MIND.
IT'S BEEN A STRANGE DAY SO FAR AND IT'S HAD ME A LITTLE ON EDGE.
AS IF THE PRESSURES OF RUNNING THE COMPANY AREN'T ENOUGH--
--WE HAD A RATHER BRUSQUE DETECTIVE DROP BY.
ASKED THE USUAL QUESTIONS AND SHOWED US SOME MARK THAT NONE OF US COULD IDENTIFY--
BUT BEFORE HE LEFT HE TOLD US WE SHOULD KEEP OUR GUARDS UP. BE CAUTIOUS OF EVERYONE, THAT SORT OF THING.
AND THEN OUR UNORTHODOX MEETING PLANS--
--WELL, IT'S ENOUGH TO GIVE ANY MAN AN UNEASY FEELING.
WELL, I HAVE TO TELL YOU, THAT CAN BE A BIT DAUNTING FOR A DOWN-TO-EARTH FELLOW LIKE MYSELF.
KNOW WHAT I MEAN, DODDS?
DODDS?

--CAN'T TELL YOU WHAT A RELIEF IT IS TO HAVE YOU WORKIN' WITH ME, MAX.

YEAH, BURKE? WHY SO?

HAD SOME REAL DICKS WITH ME THE PAST COUPLE OF DAYS.

MORE LIKELY TA *PISS* THEMSELVES THAN TO CATCH A KILLER. AT LEAST I KNOW *YOU* WON'T ACCIDENTALLY SHOOT YOURSELF IN THE FOOT OR SOMETHIN'.

YEAH, WELL, IT'S *ALWAYS* A PLEASURE TO WORK WITH YOU, BURKE.

YEAH, YOU CAN KISS *MY* SWEET ASS *TOO*, MAX.

LIEUTENANTS BURKE AND COLLINS, N.Y.P.D.

G-GOODNESS, LIEUTENANT, HAVE I DONE SOME-THING--

WE GOT A TIP THAT YOU'VE GOT A ROOM REGISTERED TO WESLEY DODDS.

Y-YES, SIR. THE LARGO SUITE, FIFTH FLOOR--

KEEP EVERYBODY AWAY FROM THAT FLOOR AND KEEP YER YAP SHUT ABOUT THIS 'TIL YOU HEAR FROM ME OTHER-WISE, UNDERSTOOD?

Y-YES. ABSOLUTELY.

YOU *HAVE* TO BE THAT ROUGH ON HIM, BURKE?

NAH, BUT HE WAS A SQUIRMER. NERVOUS. I HATE THAT IN PEOPLE. BRINGS OUT THE WORST IN ME. WHAT CAN I SAY?

GOING UP?

YEP, BUT *ALONE*. POLICE BUSINESS. TAKE THE NEXT CAR, TOOTS.

GOOD HEAVENS!

77

THE SCORPION

FINAL ACT

COME ON, DODDS! SURELY YOU CAN'T BE ASLEEP *ALREADY*; THE NIGHT'S JUST BARELY--

OH GOD... OH DEAR GOD...

DODDS?! IF YOU'RE IN HERE, AND THIS IS SOME SORT OF *PRANK* ON YOUR PART--

I CAN ASSURE YOU IT'S *NOT* FUNNY.

YOU WANT SOMETHIN' *FUNNY*, CUTLER? I GOT A *JOKE* FOR YOU.

HOW MANY WEALTHY BUSINESSMEN DOES IT TAKE T'FILL A GRAVE?

AS MANY AS YOU CAN *STUFF* IN IT.

BAM

②

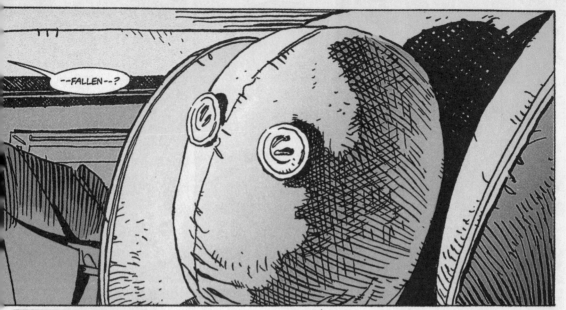

--FALLEN--?

LOOKS LIKE I'LL BE FILLIN' ONE WITH *TWO* OF YOU TONIGHT.

NOW LOOK HERE, WHATEVER YOU AND DODDS HAVE GOING ON HAS GONE FAR ENOUGH, MR.--

YOU CAN MAKE THAT SCORPION, PAL.

SCOR--? OH NO...

AND THE *ONLY* THING I'VE GOT GOING ON WITH THE QUIET *"MR. DODDS"* HERE--

--IS THAT HE'S GIVIN' ME THE PLEASURE OF KILLIN' A MAN *TWICE.*

AIN'T THAT RIGHT, *"DOLL BABY"*--?

③

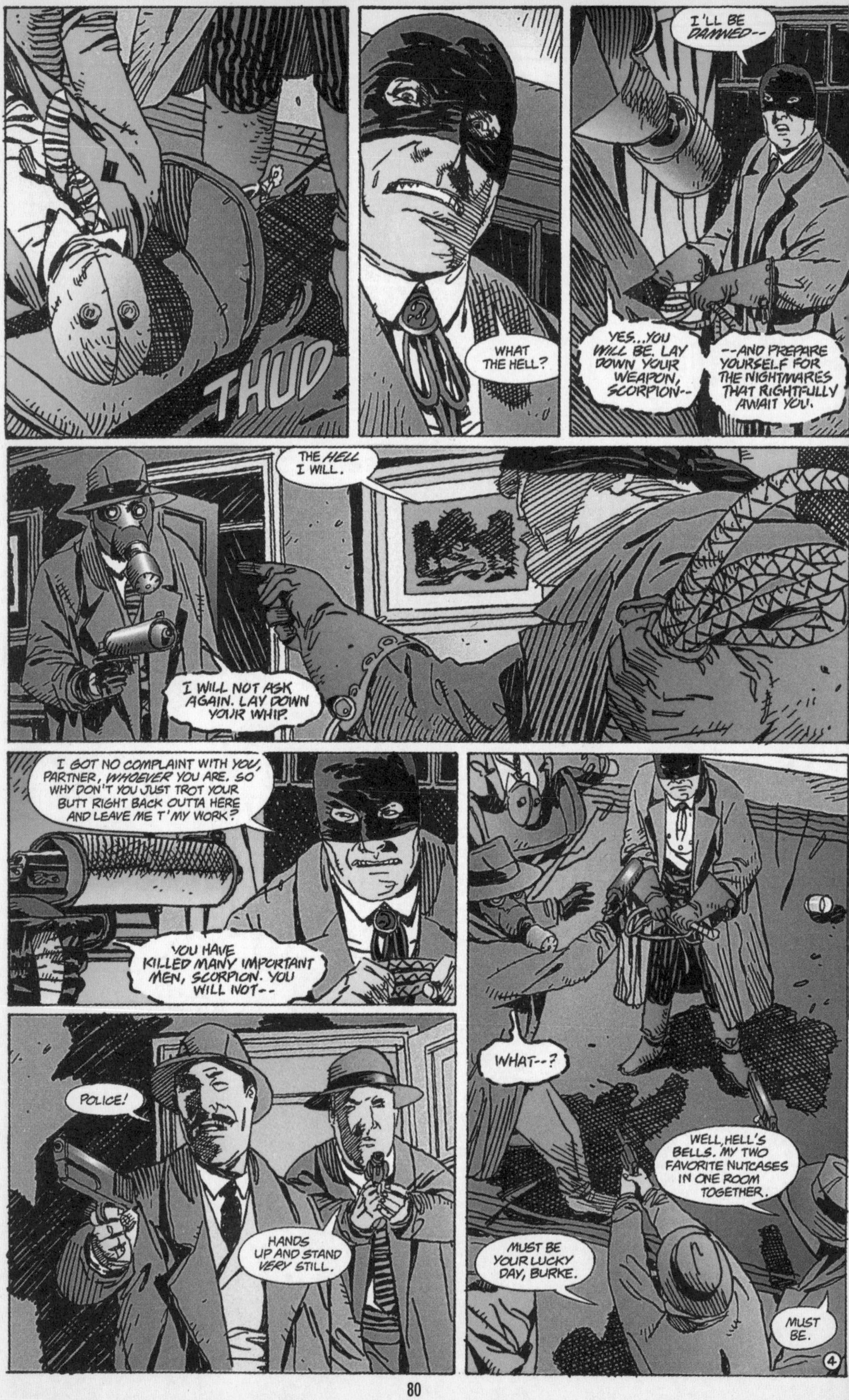
THUD
WHAT THE HELL?
I'LL BE DAMNED--
YES...YOU WILL BE. LAY DOWN YOUR WEAPON, SCORPION--
--AND PREPARE YOURSELF FOR THE NIGHTMARES THAT RIGHTFULLY AWAIT YOU.
THE HELL I WILL.
I WILL NOT ASK AGAIN. LAY DOWN YOUR WHIP.
I GOT NO COMPLAINT WITH YOU, PARTNER, WHOEVER YOU ARE. SO WHY DON'T YOU JUST TROT YOUR BUTT RIGHT BACK OUTTA HERE AND LEAVE ME T'MY WORK?
YOU HAVE KILLED MANY IMPORTANT MEN, SCORPION. YOU WILL NOT--
POLICE!
HANDS UP AND STAND VERY STILL.
WHAT--?
WELL, HELL'S BELLS. MY TWO FAVORITE NUTCASES IN ONE ROOM TOGETHER.
MUST BE YOUR LUCKY DAY, BURKE.
MUST BE.
4

DIAN? THAT YOU? LISTEN, I WON'T BE ABLE TO--TO--

DAMN IT! WHERE IS THAT *PAPER?* HERE! GOOD--UH--I WON'T BE ABLE TO--

DADDY? YOU SOUND ABSOLUTELY *HAGGARD.* WHAT'S WRONG?

SEEMS LIKE I CAN'T GET HOME THESE DAYS BEFORE I'M CALLED RIGHT BACK OUT. THE STATION JUST GOT AN UNEXPECTED BREAK ON THIS SCORPION CASE.

ANONYMOUS TIP, UH...

DADDY...YOU'RE KEEPING SOMETHING FROM ME. WHAT *IS* IT?

WELL, I SUPPOSE YOU'D FIND OUT *ANYHOW.* THE TIP WAS THAT THE SCORPION IS GOING AFTER STEPHEN CUTLER TONIGHT--

--AND WHEN THEY CONTACTED HIS OFFICE TO *WARN* HIM, HIS DAUGHTER--

CASSANDRA?

YES, CASSANDRA. SHE TOLD US THAT HER FATHER HAD GONE OFF TO A PRIVATE MEETING ...WITH *WESLEY.*

CLAC

WESLEY? BUT HE'S TOO ILL TO--DO YOU MEAN THAT HE--?

NOW, DIAN, DON'T GO GETTING ALL EXCITED, EVERYTHING WILL BE JUST FINE--

CLAC

DAMN RIGHT IT WILL, AND I INTEND TO *BE* THERE WHEN IT DOES.

DIAN--?

I'M GOING *WITH* YOU.

NOW DIAN--

LET'S GO, DADDY.

⑤

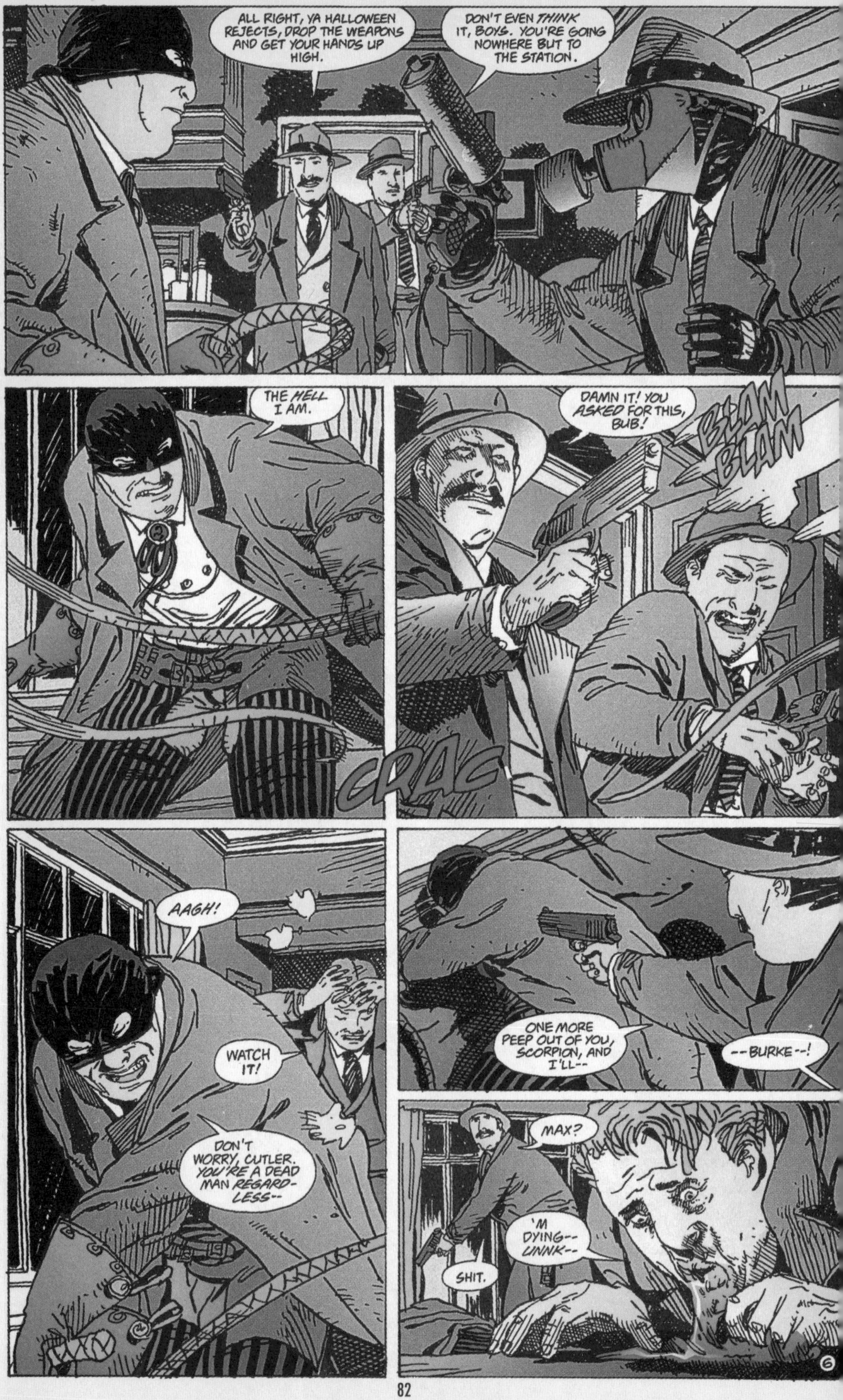
ALL RIGHT, YA HALLOWEEN REJECTS, DROP THE WEAPONS AND GET YOUR HANDS UP HIGH.
DON'T EVEN THINK IT, BOYS. YOU'RE GOING NOWHERE BUT TO THE STATION.
THE HELL I AM.
CRAC
DAMN IT! YOU ASKED FOR THIS, BUB!
BLAM BLAM
AAGH!
WATCH IT!
DON'T WORRY, CUTLER. YOU'RE A DEAD MAN REGARDLESS--
ONE MORE PEEP OUT OF YOU, SCORPION, AND I'LL--
--BURKE--!
MAX?
'M DYING-- UNNK--
SHIT.
6

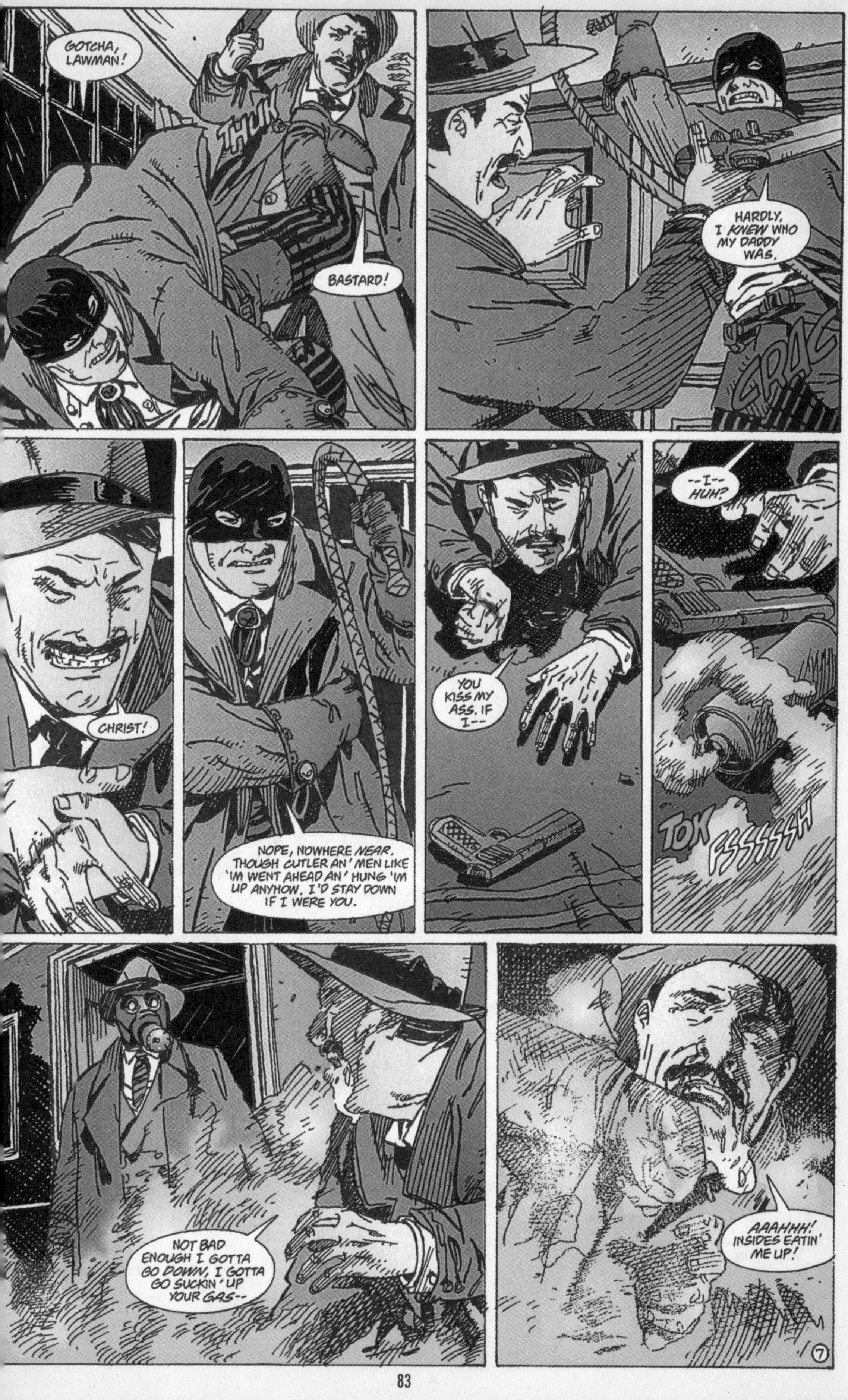
GOTCHA, LAWMAN!
THUK
BASTARD!
HARDLY. I KNEW WHO MY DADDY WAS.
CRAC
CHRIST!
NOPE, NOWHERE NEAR. THOUGH CUTLER AN' MEN LIKE 'IM WENT AHEAD AN' HUNG 'IM UP ANYHOW. I'D STAY DOWN IF I WERE YOU.
YOU KISS MY ASS. IF I--
--I-- HUH?
TOK
FSSSSSSH
NOT BAD ENOUGH I GOTTA GO DOWN, I GOTTA GO SUCKIN' UP YOUR GAS--
AAAHHH! INSIDES EATIN' ME UP!
7

YOU GOT IN MY WAY, BURKE. ∴COUGH∴ NEVER STEP ON A SCORPION.

AND AS FER YOU ∴COUGH∴ CUTLER. THERE'S STILL A STING WAITIN', COUNT ON IT.

∴COUGH COUGH∴

YOU'LL BE ALONE AGAIN SOMETIME IN THE FUTURE, BUT NOT AS ALONE AS YOU THINK.

DO NOT SURRENDER TO THE SCORPION'S STING.

HOFF! DON'T LET HIM-- AWAY--

--JESUS-- BURNIN' UP--

DON'T TRY TO MOVE. THIS WILL STOP THE POISON'S EFFECTS.

AND DON'T WORRY... THE SCORPION WILL NOT ELUDE ME.

∴COUGH∴

HUNNH!

HE WILL LEAVE A TRAIL--

NNNNN...

WHICH I WILL FOLLOW TO HIS BITTER END.

KLINN-CHKKT!

NNNH! SHIT!

EH?

DAMN IT!

THE EMBERS OF THE SCORPION'S ESCAPE ROPE FALL AWAY AS QUICKLY AND CLEANLY AS MAX'S LIFE.

THE NIGHT AIR HITS THE BACK OF MY NECK WITH A CHILL THAT IS AMPLIFIED BY THE REALIZATION THAT I HAVE PLAYED MY SURPRISE CARD, AND HAVE STILL COME UP EMPTY-HANDED.

⑨

THE DIFFICULTIES OF THIS NIGHT HAVE ONLY JUST BEGUN.

NO, NO... I'LL STOP BY MAX'S PLACE AND TELL HER... MAGGIE'D *WANT* TO HEAR IT FROM A FRIEND. *UH-HUH.* RIGHT.

SOMETHING HAPPEN, ROSS?

I'LL SAY SO, LARRY. THAT WAS OUR BACKUP MAN AT THE SCENE. THE TIP WAS DEAD ON, BUT THE WHOLE THING WENT UP IN THEIR FACES.

THE SCORPION *WAS* THERE, BUT MANAGED TO GET AWAY *AFTER* KILLING COLLINS. BURKE TOOK A LASHING TOO, BUT PULLED THROUGH IT SOMEHOW--

COLLINS? OH GEEZ, THAT'S--

WHAT ABOUT WESLEY DODDS? IS HE ALL RIGHT? OH... *AND* MR. CUTLER, OF COURSE.

CUTLER'S KNOCKED OUT, BUT OTHERWISE FINE. DODDS WASN'T EVEN THERE, THOUGH.

LOOKS LIKE *THAT* WAS JUST A SETUP TO DRAW CUTLER OUT.

THAT CAN'T *BE.* WHY WOULDN'T HE JUST GO AFTER MR. CUTLER IN HIS HOME, LIKE HE DID WITH THE OTHERS?

NOT TO MENTION THE ANONYMOUS TIP-- WHY WOULD HE GIVE HIMSELF UP?

I JUST CAN'T GET OVER POOR MAX.

YOU KNOW, THAT'S TRUE, YOUR DAUGHTER'S QUITE A LITTLE DETECTIVE, LARRY.

YEAH, WELL, NOT *TOO* SURPRISING, I GUESS, GIVEN THAT THAT *SANDMAN* CHARACTER WAS INVOLVED IN THE WHOLE BLOWUP.

THE SANDMAN, HUH?

THE SANDMAN... HM.

10

--SORRY, DAD, I'M SORRY--

--I'LL GET 'EM FOR YA--

--I'LL STILL GET 'EM--

--I'M NOT INCOMPETENT, I JUST--

-- JUST-- DAMN IT!

WELL ISN'T THIS LUCKY?

⑪

--NO, NOTHING. I JUST WANT TO... FRESHEN UP A BIT. I'LL BE RIGHT BACK.

HELLO, HUMPHRIES. I KNOW HE'S STILL *AILING*, BUT COULD YOU PROP WESLEY UP TO THE PHONE? I PROMISE I WON'T BE A MOMENT AND THEN HE CAN GET BACK TO REST.

I WOULD BE HAPPY TO, EXCEPT THAT MR. DODDS LEFT *JUST* THIS MORNING FOR PHILADELPHIA ON BUSINESS.

PHILADELPHIA? THAT CAN'T BE. HE WAS PAINFULLY ILL JUST *YESTERDAY!*

YES, WELL, HE *DOES* HAVE REMARKABLE RESTORATIVE ABILITIES, AND THE BUSINESS SEEMED *QUITE* URGENT--

FINE THEN, I'LL CALL HIM *THERE.* COULD YOU GIVE ME THE HOTEL NAME, PLEASE?

I AM ASHAMED TO ADMIT IT, BUT I NEGLECTED TO ASK MR. DODDS WHERE HE WOULD BE LODGING. IF YOU'D CARE TO CALL BACK *TOMORROW,* I MIGHT--

OH, WESLEY...

NO NO NO. THAT'S FINE. JUST TELL WESLEY TO CALL ME AS SOON AS YOU *SEE* HIM. GOOD-BYE.

12

WELL ISN'T *THIS* LUCKY?

CASSANDRA!

I *KNOW* IT WAS IMPULSIVE OF ME TO DROP BY, BUT I REALLY WANTED TO SEE YOU.

UH, I TELL YOU, CASSANDRA--I'VE BEEN *OUT* ALL DAY AN' I SMELL LIKE THE BACK END OF A PACK MULE. WHY DON'T WE MEET UP *LATER* FOR A--

TERRY, *DON'T* BE *SILLY.*

NO, *REALLY,* IF YOU WANT TO HOOK UP *LATER* FOR DINNER AND SOME DANCING--

I'M SURE I'D BE MUCH NICER COMPANY--

IF I DIDN'T *KNOW* BETTER, MR. *STETSON,* I'D SAY YOU WERE TRYING TO DUST ME OFF.

IS THAT WHAT'S HAPPENING, TERRY?

NOW DON'T BE *SILLY.* I'M JUST-- I JUST NEED SOME *TIME* TO GET MYSELF TOGETHER IS ALL.

I DON'T MIND WAITING, IN FACT I'D *LOVE* TO JUST SIT AND TALK TO YOU WHILE YOU GET READY FOR OUR NIGHT TOGETHER.

NIGHT?

OH YES. I FEEL I'VE *REALLY* COME TO KNOW YOU. THESE PAST FEW DAYS *ESPECIALLY.*

I HAVE A *VERY* SPECIAL NIGHT PLANNED.

NOW, *CASSIE*--

YOU KNOW, I'VE NEVER NOTICED THAT BOLO TIE BEFORE. WHAT AN *INTERESTING* DESIGN. HAVE YOU WORN IT TO *WORK?*

THIS?

UH...NO--

OR DO YOU *ONLY* WEAR IT TO *KILL PEOPLE?* OPEN THE *DOOR.*

13

AH GEEZ, LIEUTENANT, I'M JUST TRYIN' T' HELP HERE. YOU LOOK *REALLY* SICK~

YOU KNOW, LIEUTENANT, I DON'T THINK YOU LOOK TOO GOOD. ARE YOU SURE YOU WOULDN'T RATHER I TOOK YOU HOME?

OF COURSE I LOOK LIKE HELL. I'VE BEEN WHIPPED, POISONED, GASSED, AND SHOT FULL OF GOD KNOWS *WHAT* TONIGHT.

FUNNY THING, KEMP. I REMEMBER CALLING FOR A CAR. I DON'T REMEMBER CALLING FOR A GOD-DAMN WET NURSE.

YOU, ON THE OTHER HAND, PROBABLY HAD YOUR BIGGEST TROUBLE T'DAY WHEN THE LUNCH ROOM RAN OUTTA THEM SAUSAGE ROLLS--THAT--THA--

HURRAFFFF

I'M TELLIN'YA, SIR--

I'M TELLIN' *YOU* TO SHUT UP AND *DRIVE*. WE GOTTA GET TO STETSON'S PLACE *QUICK*, AND I'M BETTIN' WE'RE GONNA FIND HIM THERE PATCHIN' UP A NASTY FLESH WOUND.

ROSS O'DONALD. YEAH?... YEAH, SULLIVAN, SHOOT... UH HUM...YEAH, UH...WE'VE GOT HIM AT 334 EAST 75TH STREET...

...RIGHT... YEAH, I'LL GET BACK-UP IN THERE *PRONTO*.

14

THAT WAS SULLIVAN. SAYS BURKE JUST TOOK OUT OF THE HOTEL ON A JAG.

DID HE COME UP WITH SOMETHING CONCRETE?

CAN'T SAY, FOR SURE, BUT HE THINKS IT'S ONE OF THE YOUNGER GUYS AT THE COMPANY...TERRY STETSON.

I THOUGHT THEY SAID BURKE HAD BEEN HURT IN THE SCUFFLE?

YEAH, BUT YOU KNOW BURKE. SATAN HIMSELF COULDN'T HOLD THAT MAN DOWN AGAINST HIS WILL.

STILL, I DON'T THINK BURKE SHOULD CONFRONT THIS FELLA ALONE.

MILLER!

YEAH, SARGE?

GET ME THREE CARS FULL AND MEET ME AT 334 EAST 75TH.

WE GOT A POSSIBLE MAKE ON THIS SCORPION, SO MAKE SURE WE'VE GOT THE FIREPOWER TO NAIL 'IM IF WE'RE RIGHT. HE'S A TRICKY BASTARD.

YOU GOT IT, SARGE.

-- I DON'T KNOW WHAT YOU'RE TALKING ABOUT.

CASSANDRA--

YOU'RE A TALKER, TERRY. I'VE KNOWN THAT ABOUT YOU SINCE DAY ONE, BUT IT'S NOT GOING TO WORK FOR YOU THIS TIME, SO CAN IT.

15

ALL RIGHT THEN, LITTLE LADY, SINCE *YOU'RE* THE ONE WITH THE *POWER* HERE, WHY DON'T YOU DO THE TALKING AN' TELL ME WHAT YOU *WANT?*

I WANT TO KNOW *WHY.* WHY DID YOU KILL THOSE MEN? I THOUGHT YOU LIKED ME, AND YET YOU TRIED TO KILL MY OWN FATHER. WHY?

BECAUSE HE HAD IT COMIN'. THEY *ALL* DID.

HAD IT *COMING?* MY FATHER TREATED YOU LIKE A SON.

YEAH? WELL, THAT'S MIGHTY IRONIC SINCE IT WAS YOUR FATHER AND HIS BUDDIES THAT DROVE MY PA TO AN EARLY GRAVE. THEY CRUSHED HIM. *BROKE* HIM.

WHERE *I* COME FROM, YOU DON'T THROW PEOPLE'S LIVES AWAY OVER NOTHING. THEY'RE JUST GETTIN' WHAT'S COMIN' TO 'EM.

THAT STORY I TOLD YOU ABOUT MY FATHER, AND THE RAILROAD? *BULLSHIT.* MY FATHER WAS A *FARMER* IN TEXAS.

AND WE WERE PERFECTLY HAPPY UNTIL YOUR FATHER'S COMPANY SENT ITS GODDAMN OIL SURVEYORS AROUND. HE --

UNNH...

CLAC

YOU STEP AWAY FROM THAT CASE THIS *INSTANT.*

NOW, CASSANDRA, I'M NOT DOING ANYTHING WITH *THAT.* I'M JUST STEADYING MYSELF. I'VE BEEN... *HURT.*

LET ME GET THIS COAT OFF AND I'LL *SHOW* YOU.

16

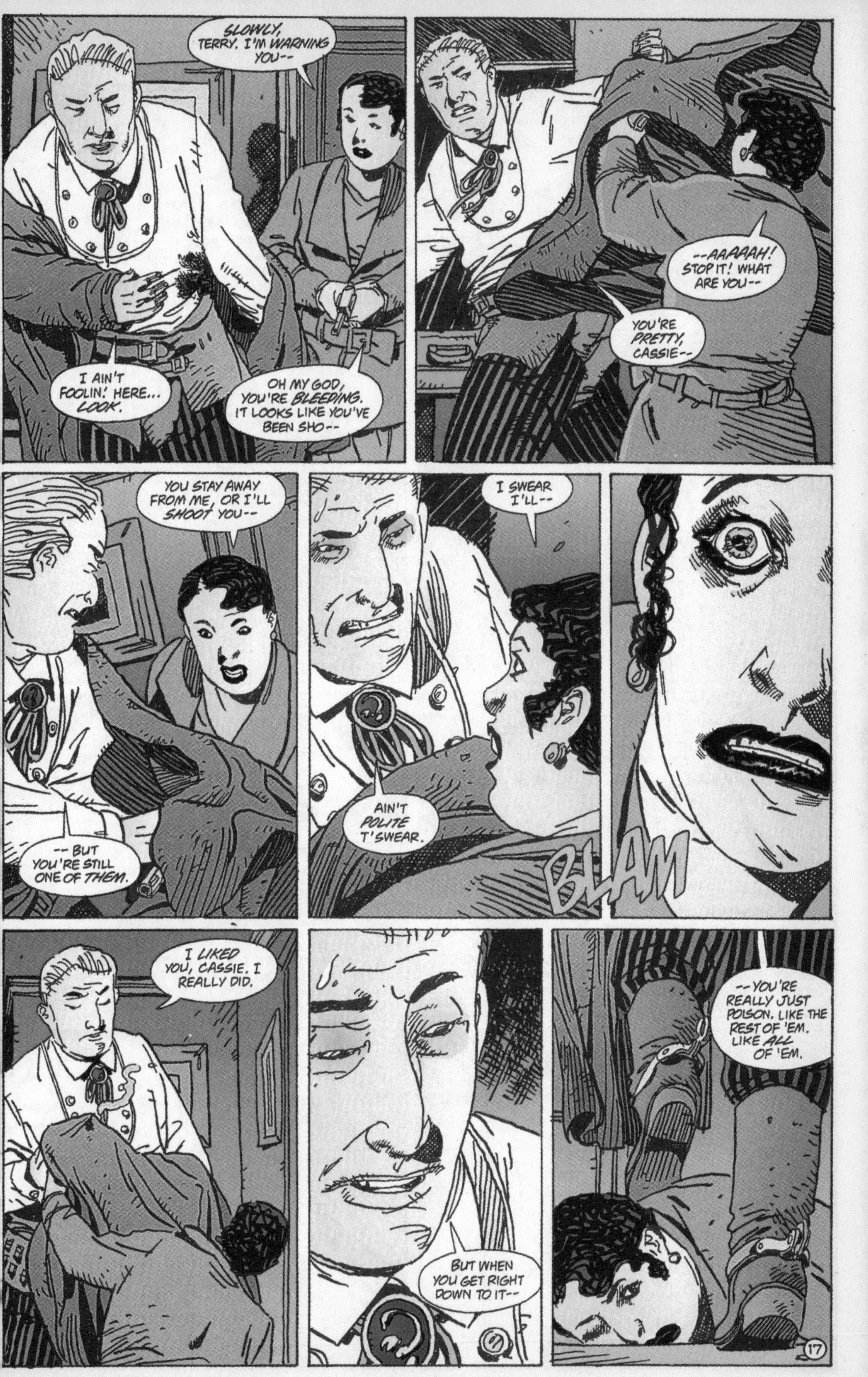
SLOWLY, TERRY. I'M WARNING YOU--
I AIN'T FOOLIN'! HERE... LOOK.
OH MY GOD, YOU'RE BLEEDING. IT LOOKS LIKE YOU'VE BEEN SHO--
--AAAAAH! STOP IT! WHAT ARE YOU--
YOU'RE PRETTY, CASSIE--
YOU STAY AWAY FROM ME, OR I'LL SHOOT YOU--
--BUT YOU'RE STILL ONE OF THEM.
I SWEAR I'LL--
AIN'T POLITE T'SWEAR.
BLAM
I LIKED YOU, CASSIE. I REALLY DID.
BUT WHEN YOU GET RIGHT DOWN TO IT--
--YOU'RE REALLY JUST POISON. LIKE THE REST OF 'EM. LIKE ALL OF 'EM.
17

NO, NO NEED TO WAIT. THANKS.

--YEAH, WELL, NO WHIP MARKS ON *THIS* DAME. LOOKS LIKE HE JUST *SHOT HER*--

EXCUSE ME. SORRY!

CASSANDRA?

NOT ANY MORE.

MIND TELLIN' ME JUST WHAT IN THE HELL *YOU'RE* DOIN' HERE, MISS BELMONT.

I KNEW HER, AND-- OH-- I WAS *SNOOPING*, I ADMIT IT. I WAS IN THE PRECINCT WITH DADDY AND OVERHEARD THE CRIME REPORT. ROSS O'DONALD SAID YOU WERE HEADED TO THIS ADDRESS.

LIEUTENANT, I THINK THE SANDMAN STAGED THIS EVENING'S EVENTS IN ORDER TO DRAW THE SCORPION OUT.

WE GOT A TIP-OFF ON THAT MEETING.

WHY WOULD A GUY BLOW HIS OWN SETUP?

MAYBE THE TIP WAS *CASSANDRA'S* DOING. SHE ACTED AS IF SHE KNEW MORE THAN SHE WAS LETTING ON WHEN I SPOKE WITH HER YESTERDAY. PERHAPS SHE UNCOVERED HIS VENDETTA.

HIS... SAY, IF HE ISN'T *HERE* THAT PROBABLY MEANS HE'S GONE AFTER LANE.

I GOTTA GET *OVER* THERE.

I'LL GO *WITH* YOU.

THE *HELL* YOU WILL.

LIEUTENANT, YOU CAN'T LEAVE THIS SCENE UNATTENDED, YOUR BACKUP HASN'T ARRIVED--

--AND YET YOU CLEARLY ARE IN NO CONDITION TO DRIVE YOURSELF.

NOT A CHANCE IN HELL, SWEETHEART.

(18)

RUDY? BE A DEAR AND BRING ME SOME *CHOCOLATES*. THIS PROKOFIEV HAS LEFT ME ABSOLUTELY *FAMISHED*.

YES, MR. LANE.

Hm hm hmmmm hm hm hmmmm

-- WILL RETURN WITH THE CONCLUSION OF "SCYTHIAN SUITE" BY SERGEI PROKOFI--

OH! RUDY? BRING ME SOME COFFEE WITH THAT. *HOT COFFEE*, RUDY!

I GOT SOMETHIN' HOT FOR YA, PARTNER--

-- AND I'M MORE THAN HAPPY TO GIVE IT TO YA.

SSSSSS

KLATCH

ZZZZ-- SNORK-- ZZZZZ

19

--TOMORROW NIGHT, JAZZ MUSIC WITH LESTER "SAWTOOTH" HAWKINS AND THE EMPIRE CITY--

JAZZ?

THAT VULGAR MUSIC HAS *NO* PLACE IN THIS CULTURE.

AN' YOU'RE JUST THE ONE TO DECIDE, WHAT BELONGS AN' WHAT *DON'T*, AIN'T YA, LANE?

WHO--?

YOU! YOU'D BETTER STAY AWAY FROM ME! MY VALET IS ON HIS WAY BACK AND --

AND HE'S AS LIKELY TO RUN IN HERE AND *SUCK* ME AS THROW ME OUT.

HOW DO-- HOW DARE YOU!

HOW DARE I WHAT? POINT OUT THE TRUTH? EVERYONE AT THE OFFICE KNOWS ALL ABOUT YOU AND YOUR HOUSEBOYS, LANE.

THE OFFICE? YOU--?

YEAH, OLD MAN. WE KNOW EACH OTHER. AN' LONGER THAN YOU *THINK*.

PLEASE--

I'M SURE THAT WHATEVER THIS IS ABOUT, WE CAN WORK IT OUT. I CAN PAY YOU ANYTHING YOU--

20

YOU CAN *PAY* ME? I *DOUBT* IT. HOW MUCH IS A MAN'S LIFE WORTH? *TWO THOUSAND? TEN THOUSAND?*

HOW MUCH WAS MY *FATHER'S* LIFE WORTH? HUH? *NOTHING?* 'CAUSE THAT'S ALL IT AMOUNTED TO.

TERRY? I-- BUT I DIDN'T *KNOW* YOUR FATHER-- I-- I DON'T KNOW ANY OTHER STETSONS--

STETSON'S A HAT. MY REAL NAME IS *PRITCHARD!* TERRY *PRITCHARD.*

NOW YOU REMEMBER, DON'T YA? TWELVE YEARS AGO YOU TALKED MY FATHER INTO SELLING OFF OUR LANDS IN TEXAS SO YOU COULD PUMP THE LIFE OUTTA IT. OUTTA *US!*

NO! NO, NO... WE PAID A *FAIR* PRICE... A *GOOD* PRICE FOR THE LAND. PRITCHARD BECAME A WEALTHY MAN. HE--

YOU GAVE HIM *MONEY,* ALL RIGHT, AND AFTER YOU WINED AND DINED HIM, YOU TREATED HIM LIKE AN OUTCAST. HE WANTED A BETTER LIFE. TO BE SOMEBODY *OUTSIDE* OF TEXAS TOO, BUT YOU REFUSED HIM THAT.

YOUR MONEY RUINED HIS LIFE! HE PISSED IT AWAY GAMBLING UNTIL HE FINALLY COULDN'T SETTLE UP ONE HOT AUGUST AFTERNOON.

MA JUST DRANK HERSELF INTO THE GRAVE.

AND-- MY SISTER--

--EMMALINE... EMMALINE WENT TO... *HOLLYWOOD!*

SWEET JESUS.

NO, YOU DIDN'T DO ANY OF THAT, LANE--

--YOUR *MONEY* DID.

SAME DIFFERENCE.

21

97

THE PATH OF YOUR POISONOUS HATRED STOPS HERE, SCORPION.

YOU AGAIN? I'LL--

SLEEP AND DREAM OF THE EVIL YOU HAVE CRUELLY WROUGHT.

FOOOOSH

HURK-- YOU AIN'T GONNA TAKE ME DOWN, LITTLE MAN.

THUD

YOU HIDE BEHIND THAT MASK LIKE THESE BASTARDS HIDE BEHIND THEIR WEALTH!

BUT WITHOUT THAT PROTECTION--

YOU'RE JUST AN-- HUKK-- ORDINARY MAN--

22

--NO DIFFERENT-- HUKFF--

--JUST A--HUKK--

NNNH--

--JUST A MAN...

...JUST A NORMAL MAN WITH A DOLLAR IN HIS HAND HE...

...HE WANTED TO BUY A PONY... A LITTLE PONY... BUT HIS DADDY...

...HIS DADDY MADE HIM... EARN IT...

MR. LANE?

...MADE HIM EARN IT DOING THINGS... HE...

...HE CAME INTO HIS ROOM WITH... A HANDFUL OF DOLLARS...

MR. LANE, IT'S ALL RIGHT NOW.

...AND HE SAID... GIVE YOU A DOLLAR IF YOU'LL KISS MY NECK...

...GIVE YOU ANOTHER DOLLAR IF YOU'LL... KISS MY SHOULDER...

OH DEAR, MR. LANE. WE'LL GET YOU SOME HELP.

23

IS MR. STETSON STILL ALIVE?

MAKE IT A DOUBLE.

DEPENDS ON YOUR DEFINITION. LOOKS LIKE HE'S HAD A STROKE OR SOMETHIN'.

WHAT ON *EARTH* DO YOU THINK HAPPENED? MR. LANE DOESN'T LOOK CAPABLE OF HARMING A MAN OF MR. STETSON'S SIZE.

NAH, THIS'S GOT *SANDMAN* WRITTEN ALL OVER IT.

YOU CAN STILL SMELL SOME OF THAT PUTRID SLEEPING GAS HE USES. ACCOUNTS FOR LANE'S MAN-SERVANT PASSED OUT DOWNSTAIRS TOO.

UH-HUH. HERE YA GO. THIS SEALS THE GOD-DAMN DEAL ALTOGETHER.

WHAT IS IT?

HE LOVES TO LEAVE THESE CUTESY LITTLE NOTES AT THE SCENE. STUPID LITTLE POEMS FOLDED UP LIKE ANIMALS. FORGET WHAT THEY'RE CALLED--

"THROUGH CURRENCY OF HUMAN SOULS--"

I HAVE DECIDED. I WILL TELL HER.

DIAN IS THE MOST PRECIOUS THING IN MY HEART, AND I CAN NO LONGER KEEP ANY PIECE OF MY LIFE CLOSED TO HER.

ORIGAMI. IT'S CALLED ORIGAMI.

T H E · E N D

VERTIGO

Matt Wagner Steven T Seagle Guy Davis

SANDMAN MYSTERY THEATRE

THE SCORPION 1 of 4

"...a sudden blur of coiled leather and the flesh opened up like a rose."

WILSON
BRUNING

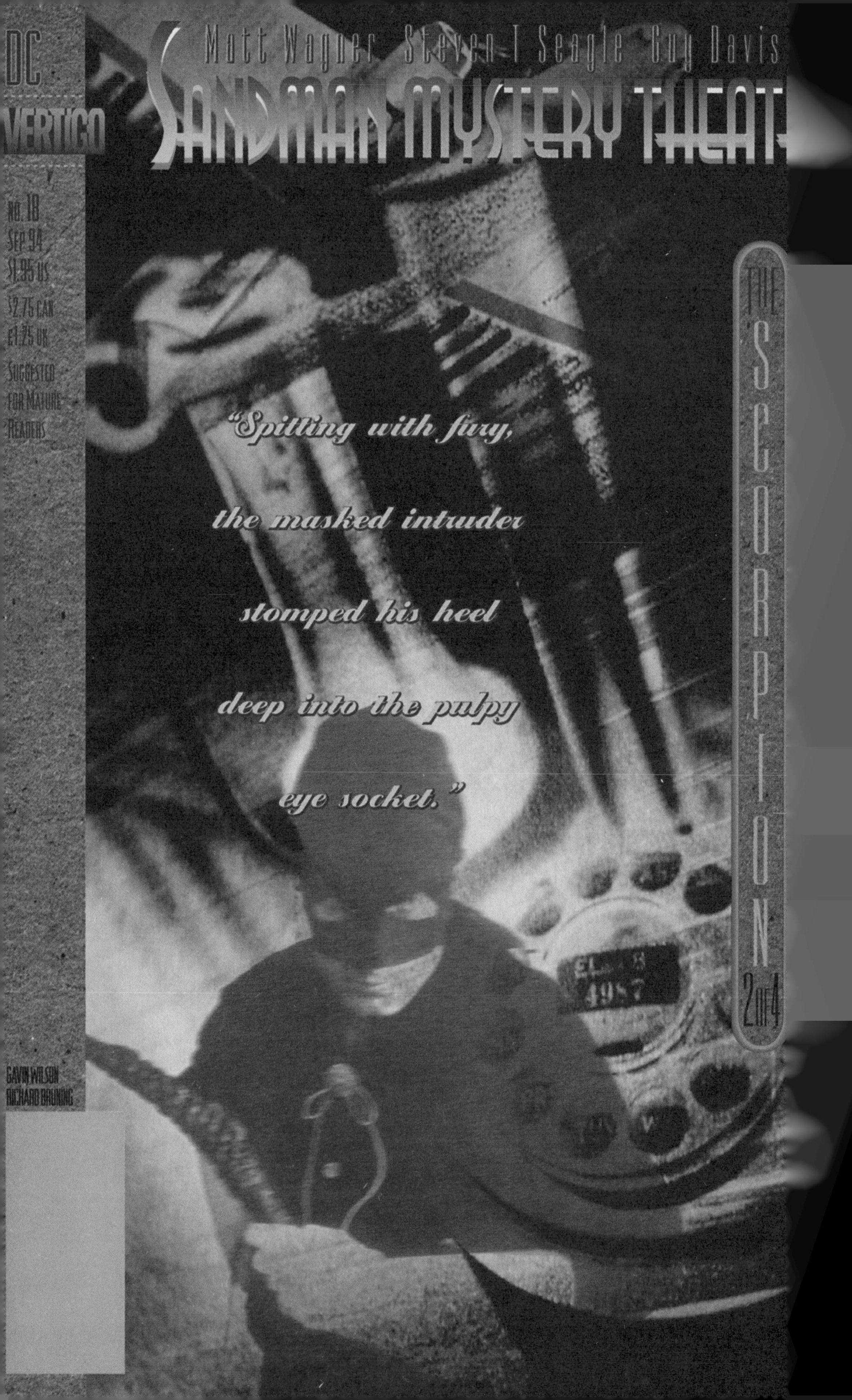
DC
VERTIGO
Matt Wagner Steven T Seagle Guy Davis
SANDMAN MYSTERY THEAT
NO. 18
SEP 94
$1.95 US
$2.75 CAN
£1.25 UK
SUGGESTED FOR MATURE READERS
"Spitting with fury, the masked intruder stomped his heel deep into the pulpy eye socket."
THE SCORPION
2 OF 4
GAVIN WILSON
RICHARD BRUNING

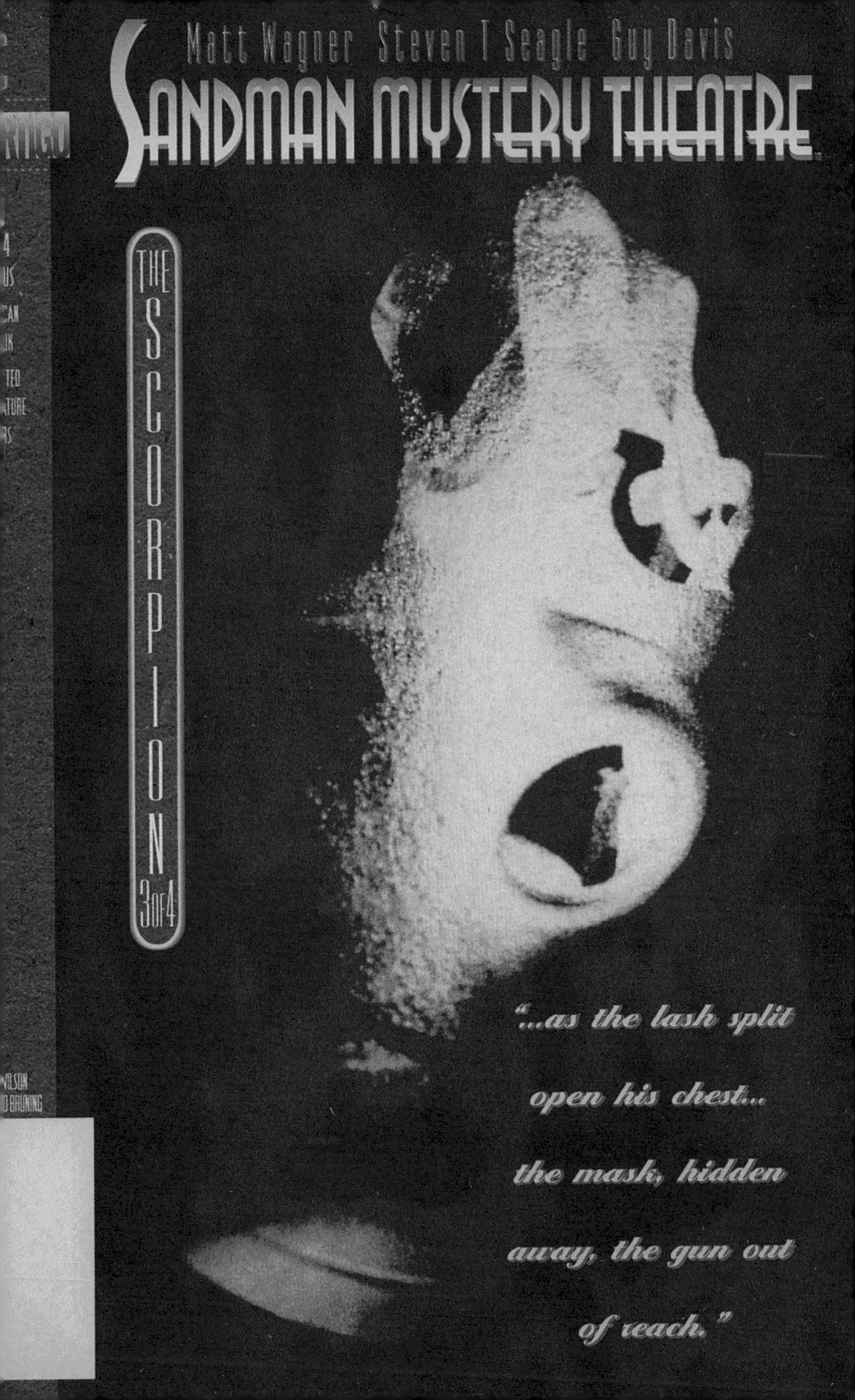
Matt Wagner Steven T Seagle Guy Davis
SANDMAN MYSTERY THEATRE
THE SCORPION
3 OF 4
"...as the lash split open his chest... the mask, hidden away, the gun out of reach."

Matt Wagner   Steven T Seagle   Guy Davis

DC VERTIGO

No. 20
Nov 94
$1.95 US
$2.75 CAN
£1.25 UK

Suggested
for Mature
Readers

Gavin Wilson
Richard Bruning

SANDMAN MYSTERY THEATRE

"..the sudden smell of sulphur

as her eyes shot steely,

cold death.."

THE SCORPION

4 of 4